A Destiny Defined

Dante Gabriel Rossetti and Elizabeth Siddal in Hastings

Jenny Ridd (photo: Peter Marsden)

A Destiny Defined

Dante Gabriel Rossetti and Elizabeth Siddal in Hastings

Jenny Ridd

Edgerton Publishing Services

Pett, East Sussex

First published in Great Britain in 2008 by
Edgerton Publishing Services
Jasmine Cottage, Elm Lane, Pett, Hastings, East Sussex TN35 4JD
Tel. +44 (0) 1424 813003
Email enquiries@eps-edge.demon.co.uk

ISBN-13: 978-9548390-4-8
ISBN-10: 0-9548390-4-8

A CIP catalogue record for this book is available from the British Library.

Typeset in Garamond by Edgerton Publishing Services.

Printed and bound in Great Britain by CPI Antony Rowe, Chippenham, Wiltshire

Every effort has been made to trace and acknowledge ownership of copyright of the illustrations used in this book. The publisher will be pleased to make suitable arrangements to clear permission with any copyright holders whom it has not been possible to contact.

Picture on front cover: Portrait of Elizabeth Siddal (1829–62) 1854 (watercolour on paper) by Dante Charles Gabriel Rossetti (1828–82). Delaware Art Museum, Wilmington, USA/F.V. DuPont Acquisition Fund/The Bridgeman Art Library

Picture on back cover: Hastings Beach with Fishing Boats, (watercolor, ca. 1850) by Barbara Leigh Smith Bodichon. Mark Samuels Lasner Collection, on loan to the University of Delaware Library

To my Grandchildren

Ben, Isabelle, and Austin

with my love and blessings

'The gift is small, the love is all'

'Perhaps there is no pleasanter watering-place in England . . . than Hastings on the Sussex Coast.'

Christina Rossetti

Contents

Introduction vii

Acknowledgements viii

1   The Rossetti House 1

2   The Rising Star 18

3   Why Hastings? 30

4   Hastings – The Halcyon Days 44

5   The Intervening Years 70

6   Return to Hastings 77

     Select Bibliography 87

Introduction

This book is not intended as a serious academic commentary for those interested in the world of art, but as a lighter read for anyone who holds a fascination for the Pre-Raphaelite characters, and the story of their visits to Hastings. That they chose Hastings is no surprise, because, then as now, the scenery is stunningly beautiful and was bound to influence and inspire any budding young artist. Thankfully images like 'Our English Coasts' (Strayed Sheep) are still familiar to us today, and I find it difficult to stand on the cliffs at Fairlight on a fine day without thinking of Holman Hunt and that rich and wonderful Pre-Raphaelite legacy.

I have focused on Gabriel Rossetti and Elizabeth Siddal, because in my seven years of living at 5 High Street, I was, in a sense, living with them. I thought about them a great deal – not as artists, but as young people in love. Their relationship was in its first flush, and they were starry-eyed with romance. I suspect that this accounted for how Lizzie was suddenly able to overcome her bouts of illness, and experience instant bursts of energy.

Yet there were others who visited Hastings who also came under the Pre-Raphaelite banner, and I had to make some reference to them, however small. Christina, Gabriel's sister, stayed in Hastings for six months during one visit, and returned several times, a fuller account of which may be found in Frances Thomas's excellent biography *Christina Rossetti*. Gabriel's brother, William, and the Rossetti parents, Gabriele and Frances, all knew Hastings as an interesting place, and as a venue for recovery from illness. And of course, no story would be complete without mention of the PRB – the Pre-Raphaelite Brotherhood, which Rossetti helped to found along with William Holman Hunt and John Everett Millais and others.

But ultimately it was Lizzie and Gabriel's lives that I became fascinated by, and wanted to delve more deeply into, in order to uncover the details of their stay in Hastings. And nobody had done it before, it seemed. I hope during this account I have put that right.

Jenny Ridd
April 2008

Acknowledgements

There are many people who have helped me through this project, offered their support and interest, and have believed in me during the journey. My heartfelt thanks go out to you all, and please forgive me for any unintentional oversights.

My list must start with two most influential men to whom I am indebted. My special thanks go to David Penfold, my wise and painstaking publisher, with whom working has been both a pleasure and a privilege. Important also has been my patient husband, Peter Marsden, for showing me the way, for assuring me I could do it, and for his contribution of quality photographs.

Further afield, I want to thank Christopher Whittick, Senior Archivist, East Sussex Record Office, who gave his time for research and lively discussion; Victoria Williams, Cathy Walling and their colleagues, Hastings Museum and Art Gallery, for prints and local information; Jan Marsh, Rossetti expert, for thoughts about DGR's poetry, inspiration, and visiting 5 High Street; Kate Perry at Girton College for sight of original documents; Anne Drewery for enthusiasm and knowledge of the Pre-Raphaelites; Steve Gooch, Playwright, and Christine Kimberely, Director, for *British Beauty*; Adrian Sumner for huge expertise and knowledge of Pre-Raphaelite art; David and Barbara Martin for house history and architecture; Karen Beauchamp, Cole and Son, for information and dating of wallpapers; Rosie Harness for details on psychology; Pam Hirsch for encouragement and visiting the Rossetti House; Jenny McDonald for reading early drafts and for support throughout; Members of HAARG for their archaeological prowess, especially the late Mike Greenhalgh; Rev. Iain Morrison for permission to re-erect the Elphick gravestone; Barry Johnson for books and information on Violet Hunt; Ralfe Whistler for hospitality and access to the Whistler family records; Dr Dennis T. Lanigan and Mark Samuels Lasner for the pictures of Lizzie from their private collections and to the latter for the picture by Barbara Leigh Smith Bodichon on the back cover; all friends who have offered encouragement and support along the way; and finally, my dear mother-in-law, Sylvia Winder, who, aged 92, has shown constant enthusiasm, interest and levity.

Picture Credits

The photographs in the book have been kindly supplied from the following: Ashmolean Museum, Oxford; Bridgeman Art Library; Department of Rare Books & Special Collections, Princeton University Library; Dr Dennis T. Lanigan Collection, Canada; Fitzwilliam Museum, Cambridge; Hastings Museum and Art Gallery; Mark Samuels Lasner Collection, University of Delaware; East Sussex Record Office; Mistress and Fellows, Girton College, Cambridge; Past Historic Trust Archive; Personal Collection of J. Ridd & P. Marsden; Peter Marsden; Victoria and Albert Museum; National Portrait Gallery; Violet Hunt's *The Wife of Rossetti* uncredited photo.

1

The Rossetti House

As the last screw bit into the brickwork, we stood back and admired our handiwork. We had recently commissioned a new blue plaque for our house at 5 High Street, Hastings, and were affixing it proudly to the front of our property.

Instead of commemorating the arrival of one famous Pre-Raphaelite artist a hundred and fifty years ago, we were celebrating the visit of two. The previous blue plaque had memorialised only the stay of Dante Gabriel Rossetti at the house in 1854, and had completely ignored the fact that his muse and inspiration, Elizabeth Siddal, had been there too.

The recent white timber boarding and tiled front of 5 High Street today masks the 200 year old timber frame house behind (Past Historic Archive)

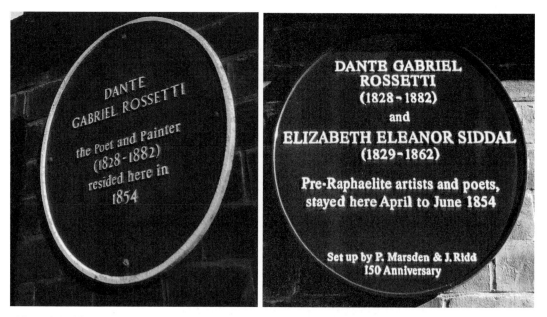

The original blue plaque (on the left) began our quest for what really happened there in 1854, while our new plaque (on the right) commemorated the 150th anniversary of Lizzie and Gabriel's stay in the house, and recognises Elizabeth Siddal as an artist in her own right (Past Historic Archive)

Siddal later became Rossetti's wife and a budding artist, and has at last now achieved acclaim as a Pre-Raphaelite painter in her own right. Our new plaque recognised this important fact, and gave her parity.

However, it seems that history has twisted the story a little. Gabriel Rossetti had indeed stayed there for a short while, but it was Lizzie Siddal who spent several weeks there, recuperating in the resort, drawing, and generally regaining her strength – and it was she who was the sole reason for Rossetti's visit.

For us, it had all begun with finding, and buying, 5 High Street in 1997. Its prestigious blue plaque had not been my main focus as I eyed the obvious amount of interior decoration needed to make the place habitable. But my husband Peter Marsden, ever the historian and archaeologist, immediately saw the historical potential of renovating such a property, and thus we began the research alongside the makeover, embarking on the steepest learning curve of our lives.

As we came to know 5 High Street, so the house yielded up its astonishing secrets to us. We gradually realised that this very ordinary house was, in fact, quite extraordinary. We found ourselves delving into what turned out to be an amazing historical legacy.

Rarely in this country has research been carried out in such depth on such an ordinary house. Whilst more elite bodies like English Heritage and the National Trust

Dante Gabriel Rossetti (self-portait, 1855, pen & indian ink and brown ink on paper;
Fitzwilliam Museum, University of Cambridge, UK/The Bridgeman Art Library)

protect our grander castles, stately homes and manor houses, seldom do smaller properties attract the same amount of attention unless someone famous had lived there.

In the case of 5 High Street, someone famous had visited. The moment Rossetti and Siddal crossed the threshold of Number 5, they became an integral part of its history and, as we followed their trail, so we became a part of the drama – and so began the story of us uncovering the story of them. During the research our emotions ranged from wildly excited by any new discoveries, to highly frustrated when the scent went cold. Meanwhile, the archive grew – and grew.

In order to understand the artwork executed by Rossetti and Siddal, we attended a study weekend in Chester organised by Chester City Council and, for 48 hours, we

Elizabeth Eleanor Siddal, (by Dante Gabriel Rossetti, 1855, pen and ink on paper; Ashmolean Museum, University of Oxford, UK/The Bridgeman Art Library)

steeped ourselves in everything Pre-Raphaelite. At the same time, we caused a slight stir amongst our fellow course members when we told them where we lived.

A coach took us to the Walker Art Gallery in Liverpool, the Lady Lever Gallery in Port Sunlight Village, and to George Melly's Sudely House, where we feasted on Pre-Raphaelite art. We attended several hours of lectures given by the then Arts Development Officer for Chester, Adrian Sumner, whose enthusiasm filled our senses with the feast of rich colour, mystique and magnificence that is Pre-Raphaelitism.

We saw further Pre-Raphaelite Brotherhood (PRB) exhibitions at the Tate, at the Royal Academy and in Southampton. Jan Marsh, biographer of both Rossetti and

Siddal, had sought to redress the position of Pre-Raphaelite women and, as well as writing several books, she had organised the exhibition 'Pre-Raphaelite Women Artists', at the art galleries in Manchester, Birmingham and Southampton.

After reading Jan Marsh's books, I corresponded with her and invited her to visit us at 5 High Street. She was thrilled to see the house, especially Lizzie's room, and credited us in her biography *Dante Gabriel Rossetti Poet and Painter*. Thereafter, Jan was helpful with odd details and always an inspiration to me through her writings and exhibitions.

In 1998 a local playwright, Steve Gooch, rang me to say that he was writing a play about Barbara Lee Smith and Lizzie Siddal called *A British Beauty*. I invited him and his director wife, Christine Kimberely, to come and look over the house. Steve's play was to be performed after the unveiling ceremony of a blue plaque, which had just been put up on 9 Pelham Crescent in honour of Barbara Leigh Smith, Rossetti's artist friend.

On the afternoon of the ceremony, we stood amongst the crowd listening to an opening speech by Charles Moore, former editor of the *Daily Telegraph* and descendant of Barbara Leigh Smith. Afterwards, I chatted to a lady next to me and discovered she

The unveiling of the blue plaque commemorating Barbara Leigh Smith Bodichon with Pam Hirsch, centre, and Charles Moore, left (Past Historic Archive)

was Pam Hirsch, author of *Barbara Leigh Smith Bodichon, Feminist, Artist and Rebel.* Following the ceremony, Pam and several others squeezed into our dining hall at 5 High Street to enjoy an impromptu fish and chip supper before we all attended Steve Gooch's play at St Mary in the Castle, Pelham Crescent, a few doors down from Barbara Leigh Smith's house.

During the performance, I was delighted to note that one of the character's lines referred to the dark narrow corridor of Number 5, and how the sound carried inside the house. Steve had added these few lines after visiting the house, and had acquired a feel for what it would have been like in Lizzie's day.

We read and read, watched videos and listened to Radio 4 plays, joined the Pre-Raphaelite Society, and did anything else that pertained to the Pre-Raphaelites. All the time we were building a greater awareness of Lizzie and Gabriel. As we uncovered more details about the house, and as we searched the local records, we began to see a clearer picture of their visit to Hastings. We followed in their footsteps and visited the local places they had seen. We were almost disbelieving at the fact that Lizzie had been near death one day, yet with Gabriel's arrival she had recovered sufficiently to manage the extremely steep incline of the East Hill the very next day. This is a cliff, with a slope that would be problematic for the incapacitated or faint-hearted, so how had she managed to climb it? We climbed, with some difficulty, towards the arches on which they had carved their initials, but were disappointed to find that wind and weather had eroded them.

Sarah Veness was landlady Mrs Elphick's servant at 5 High Street in 1854 and, although my discovery of Sarah Veness as Barbara Leigh Smith's neighbour may be only a small one, I was greatly excited by it. When we read of the Chatfields in Violet Hunt's *The Wife of Rossetti*, and were able to trace them through local census records, we were elated. When we further realised that the Chatfields had been the only witnesses at Lizzie and Gabriel's wedding, it was a major coup. These were people who add substance to the story, and hopefully they will not be ignored in future. I hope that actually living in the house, and my perspective of Hastings, will contribute to a greater understanding of events.

It was Violet Hunt who gave us the description of landlady Mrs Elphick's wallpaper at Number 5. Imagine the thrill of finding a layer of wallpaper – one of eight layers – that not only fitted the description, but, when dated by a wallpaper expert, exactly matched the time of Lizzie and Gabriel's visit.

One of the most entertaining pieces of our research was finding out who the often-mentioned Mrs Elphick was. She and her family were well documented in the local parish registers and, on discovering that her grave still existed in All Saints churchyard, we decided on an expedition to find it. We set off armed with spades, secateurs, gardening gloves, trowels, pens and paper.

Sadly, All Saints churchyard is very overgrown and, despite having a map plotting the exact position of the Elphick grave, we could not locate it when we arrived at the spot. Peter looked round the churchyard, whilst I looked again and again at the map. Then I had a 'eureka' moment, when I realised from its position that the headstone had fallen over face first, and become overgrown with vegetation. I hailed Peter and together we hacked and chopped at grass, stinging nettles and brambles until we had cleared the back of the stone. With a strength we didn't know we possessed, we levered up the gravestone until we could peer underneath and read the inscription.

It was indeed the Elphick gravestone, underneath which was a nest of slow worms. Being a tad timorous of snakes, I almost turned and fled, leaving a very red-faced Peter straining to hold up the whole weight of the stone! Once we had ascertained that it was the right stone, we then needed permission from the Rector to re-erect it.

The author and her husband, Peter Marsden, with the re-erected gravestone of Mrs Elphick, landlady to Lizzie and Gabriel. The tombstone had broken and fallen, but is now firmly cemented into the ground in All Saints Churchyard (Past Historic Archive)

Gabriel drew Lizzie at her bedroom window in 1854, the window that survives to this day (see picture on facing page). Having a half net curtain, as seen in Gabriel's pictures, gives privacy from people walking on the high pavement opposite, yet allows in the light (Elizabeth Siddal, pen and ink drawing by Dante Gabriel Rossetti; May 1854; Victoria & Albert Museum, London, UK/The Bridgeman Art Library)

His concern was that it would topple and injure passers-by, so he wanted it set in concrete. Our next churchyard expedition saw us pushing a wheelbarrow heavily laden with cement, water, spades and several cameras across a busy main road and up the steep incline of the graveyard path. Once cemented in place, we photographed each other leaning on the headstone as though we had bagged some rare trophy. And, of course, we had.

The window against which Lizzie posed as it is today

We had always teased people about the two ghosts supposedly in residence at Number 5, although we had never been given the slightest reason to believe in their existence. Peter regaled a young carpet layer with the stories as he prepared to re-carpet our bedroom, once Lizzie's room. Later the carpet fitter admitted to being a bit 'spooked'. by one of the closet doors repeatedly swinging open as he knelt on the floor. We chuckled, but didn't tell him about the one floorboard, which, when stood on in a particular position, triggered the mysterious opening!

Many times, as I went into that bedroom, I thought of Lizzie and, as I lay in bed reading books about her, it was a strange feeling to be reading accounts of her in that same room 150 years previously. If only the walls could talk . . . The room is altered today, with plasterboard covering the original beams and hiding the fireplace. The floor has been raised twice to protect a weak ceiling in the dining hall below. When Lizzie posed against the window frame for Gabriel, her height came halfway up it. I am three inches smaller at 5' 4" and yet stand further up the frame because of the raised floor levels.

We wanted to take off the boarding and uncover the fireplace that Lizzie saw and used, but were not sure that it was still there after the extensive renovations to the house 50 years ago. The original plaster walls were in such poor condition everywhere else that we decided against it. Had we done so, the lower part of the fireplace would have stood in a sort of well below the twice-raised floor.

We always had a sense of Lizzie and Gabriel being there and, accordingly, we hung his prints on every wall. Although the house had no name, everyone, including the postmen, knew it as the 'Rossetti House'. And so we came to feel that we were 'living with Rossetti'.

There is no doubt that Rossetti and Siddal's visit raised the profile of 5 High Street, and gave it status. Those interested in Pre-Raphaelitism will, of course, be familiar with the address, but it is the extraordinary wealth of documentation, and other information that they don't know about, which makes this small, vernacular dwelling so exceptional.

Although of lesser interest in the context of this Pre-Raphaelite story, some of the other historical details that we uncovered are fascinating nonetheless. For instance, deeds exist for Number 5 back to 1659 and continue in a complete run until the present day, showing signatures of former owners. And, because those owners and their tenants did interesting jobs, or were instrumental in the growth of the town, further documentation about them exists in Hastings Library, the Museum and the East Sussex County Record Office in Lewes. Gravestones are still in churchyards and prints and photographs have survived.

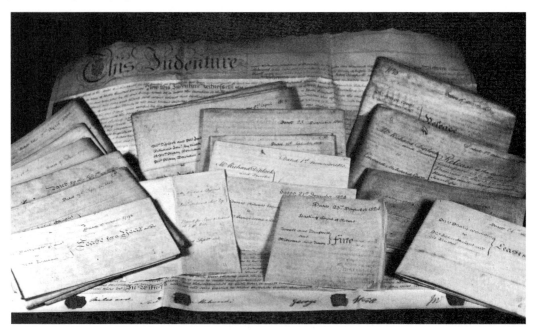

Almost 350 years of deeds for 5 High Street have provided a wealth of information about the inhabitants of the present house and the two former cottages (Past Historic Archive)

Little by little, over seven years we gathered information from all these different sources. We know that the first owner was John Akehurst, in 1620, and he had been Mayor of Hastings. Emery Taylor was the town gunner in 1699, and tested firearms in the back yard. Thomas Moore was a merchant undoubtedly made rich by smuggling and owned seven other houses besides 5 High Street. He and his wife lived elsewhere, but, when he died in 1741, his wife moved in. We discovered that Mary Wenham's complete rebuild of Number 5 in the late 1790s was done on the ill-gotten gains of smuggling. George Wooll set up a 'Repository of Arts' after Ackermann in 1823, became a publisher of lithographs and employed the now well-known Devonian artist, George Rowe, to do his artwork. Ann White was transported to Australia for seven years in 1825 for stealing three packs of cards worth 15 shillings from George Wooll's shop.

Countess Waldegrave owned 5 High Street for 50 years after George Wooll, did no repairs and left the very dilapidated house to her stableman, William Tyrell, in her will. In the 1950s Alexis Taggart owned the house. He was a musician extraordinaire, played in a local band, conducted the local orchestra and played bit parts in films with Jessie Matthews. And we bought the house from Marshall Coombes, Morris dancer and reviver of Hastings' ever-popular May Day 'Jack In The Green' festival. For many

Hastings from the White Rock. 5 High Street was the artists' centre in Hastings during the 1820s when George Wooll had his 'Repository of Arts' there, from which he published many lithographs of fashionable places in Sussex (Personal Collection of J. Ridd & P. Marsden)

The annual Jack-in-the-Green procession, celebrating the coming of Spring and the rebirth of the earth, had its beginnings partly at 5 High Street, seen here in the background (Past Historic Archive)

years Jack was built in the back garden of Number 5, and legend has it that he is the peculiar conical shape he is because that was the only way he would go through the back gate!

These are wonderfully rich stories gleaned from surviving documentation, and are the stuff of another book. But alongside these there was also the archaeology. Very few homeowners have full-blown excavations in their back gardens – but then, not everyone is married to an archaeologist. An excavation led by Peter on the garden of Number 5 proved exceptional, with an unusually large haul of artefacts, which in turn provided vast amounts of information on the former occupants. More was found than from all other previous digs in the area collectively.

Peter saw the archaeological excavation as a way of dealing with a garden that needed a lot of attention. Grim, grey concrete covered much of it. A landscape company seemed the easy option, but Peter took the opportunity to invite members of HAARG (Hastings Area Archaeological Research Group) instead, and eight volunteers dug for eight hours a day for eight weeks.

Our archaeological excavation in the garden of 5 High Street was a popular visitor attraction during 'Old Hastings Week' 2000 (Past Historic Archive)

We struck the jackpot, except that our treasure had no monetary value whatsoever. Neighbours and friends were very supportive and, during an Old Town Week, we opened the garden to visitors. Five hundred inquisitive people called in to the back garden of Number 5 to see what was going on. Even Peter was surprised by the sheer quantity of what we took out of the ground. In his entire career he had never excavated such a large quantity of objects in one dig.

Artefacts representing 400 years of occupation on that site were found, the most significant of which were the possessions of Thomas and Joanna Moore. Their daughters, Mary and Jane, cleared the house after Joanna's death in 1757 and, with no dustbins, they dug two large pits outside the kitchen door and dropped their mother's cast-offs into it. Many items went in whole and only broke as they hit the bottom.

Peter and I spent the evenings of the whole of one winter doing 3D jigsaws, reassembling and gluing the artefacts back together again. Almost whole pots, plates, bowls, dishes, cups, mugs, glasses, teapots, pipes and wine bottles gathered before our eyes. Coins and jetons were found, as well as buttons, and glass, brick and lead from the original house. A fragment of a sundial from about 1610–20 was found, which must have been used by the very first occupier.

I did not expect to find any artefacts connected with Rossetti. After all, he was only a visitor and was there for such a short time. But whilst no Rossetti paintbrushes emerged, an old Wedgwood toilet bowl from the original outhouse was excavated – which, of course led to much ribald 'lavatory' humour from other people. However, when a member of a group of historic toilet experts dated the ceramic lavatory for us, it was we who had the last laugh. Indeed, the toilet bowl had been present in the outhouse at the time of Rossetti and Siddal's visit. They must have availed themselves of this very facility! It was this same outhouse in which Mrs. Elphick, their landlady, had placed charcoal to deaden the smell.

Today the cracked and battered artefact has been included in several talks and exhibitions, and has raised many a titter, especially when audiences read the attached label, 'Rossetti sat here'. Surely few collectors of PRB memorabilia can own such a bizarre connection to the artist?

Through the archaeology, the story of previous residents emerged. Because of accurate dating, artefacts could be linked to specific people and their lifestyles could be reconstructed. The garden had acted as a time capsule from another age. Struck by this idea, Peter buried a bagful of pre-decimalisation pennies when we put the garden back together again. 'That'll confuse them when they dig this up in the future', he said, smiling.

In 2004 the *Antiques Roadshow* visited Hastings, and we were invited along. We met

John Sandon and were televised showing off part of our collection. Whilst John deemed it worthless in monetary terms, he agreed that it was an important collection historically. There was a little father–son rivalry before filming, as Henry Sandon, (John's father) told us he was very envious of John because Henry's first love was archaeology and he would really have enjoyed working with us!

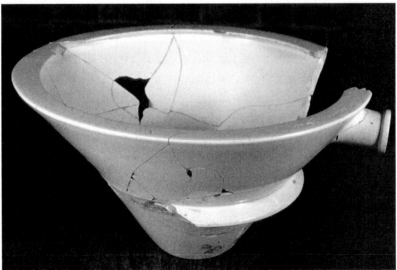

The toilet bowl of about 1800 for a flush toilet used in the garden outhouse until the 1860s, when it was broken up and buried. This would have been used by Gabriel and Lizzie and others who stayed at the house (Past Historic Archive)

We approached Hastings Museum to see if they would take the collection, but they faced the same crisis as every other museum today – lack of space. We were adamant that the collection should stay intact, the archaeology alongside the documentation, to give it context. So we set up the *Past Historic Charitable Trust*, with ourselves and two other professionals as Trustees, and this now owns the complete archive. This will allow us to raise monies for further research, conservation of objects, soil sampling, etc. It would sadden us to think that this wonderful accumulation of Hastings history did not stay in the town, since there has been enormous continuing local interest. We still give illustrated talks and lectures to societies as far away as Canterbury.

Architectural secrets were revealed too, during our renovation of the house, when it offered up several layers of period wallpapers, boarding, a plank with initials on, a medieval beam, a doorjamb from a Georgian door and so on. The archive continued to grow.

Lastly, there was the oral tradition. We taped a former owner recalling her own renovations of Number 5 in the 1950s, who remembered hearing the story of a murder committed in the kitchen during the late 1700s. An elderly builder remembered changing the original appearance of the house for ever by adding mathematical tiles and weatherboarding to the front exterior.

These are some of the characters who have inhabited 5 High Street for nearly 400 years and who have stamped their mark on it, but they are not the ones who are remembered. They were the ordinary folk who were reflective of their period, went about their daily lives, got married, had children, worked, died and were buried. The story of the house may start with post-Elizabethan England, but it took a visit by a famous artist to raise it to present-day consciousness.

Violet Hunt, in her biography of Lizzie Siddal in 1932, wrote 'Number 5 was a very old house . . .'. During their stay Lizzie and Gabriel would have been familiar with its delightful idiosyncrasies – its sloping roofs, crooked stairs, hidden closets, uneven levels, and its beautiful, unimpeded outlook over the ever green, expansive East Hill.

I believe that Peter and I were meant to buy, and uncover, the secrets of 5 High Street. He is an archaeologist, historian and writer, while I am an educationalist, historian and writer. Our discoveries were an adventure for us, and were usually rollicking good fun. On our journey we met scores of new people and made lots of new contacts. After one of our lectures, a woman said to me, 'What a privilege to have gone through all of this'. She was right, for not only have we unearthed four centuries of Hastings history, and added information to the local scene, but we have also placed 5 High Street into a national setting. After all, the house was centre stage for the story of a young couple who were to influence a new art movement throughout Britain and we are proud to give it the recognition it deserves.

This is not a story about Lizzie and Gabriel's art, but about their history and about the house that they stayed in. It is a detailed uncovering of their 1854 visit to 5 High Street, Hastings, two young people who were very much in love and who were safely cocooned in their own bubble of happiness, blissfully unaware of what lay ahead of them.

2

The Rising Star

They exhumed her late one Tuesday evening; five men in coats as dark as the night stood over her grave on a hill in Highgate Cemetery. Two began to dig by the light of a large fire burning to cleanse the surrounding air of any released toxins. It was 5 October 1869.

While two workmen from the Blackfriars Company shovelled earth, they were observed by three professional men. The first was Charles Augustus Howell, Rossetti's friend and associate; the second was Dr Llewellyn Williams, a medical man; and the third was Henry Virtue Tibbs, a lawyer hired in order to verify to the Cemetery Authorities what was being removed from the grave.

These men were overseeing the exhumation of Elizabeth Eleanor Rossetti, formerly Siddal, the late wife of the Pre-Raphaelite painter and poet, Dante Gabriel Rossetti.

Having opened the coffin, one of the men reached in and removed a small grey calf-bound book, which was hidden and entwined with what had always been Lizzie's crowning glory – her red-gold hair. The book was handed to Dr Williams, Tibbs having ascertained that it was what they were seeking. The book was 'soaked through and through' and Dr. Williams knew that not all of the writing would be decipherable, even after his ministrations of disinfecting and drying it out page by page.

This scene was possibly one of the most bizarre stories ever to come out of literary history. The book being exhumed belonged to Gabriel Rossetti and contained some of his best ever early poetry. On the day of Lizzie's funeral on 17 February 1862, driven by overwhelming remorse and impulsive momentum, Gabriel had placed the little book of poems into the coffin with her in an extravagant gesture of atonement.

And yet two weeks after the exhumation, he was in possession of the book and able to copy out his work again, seven and a half years after he had buried it. It was a grisly task and, understandably anxious and tortured by self-reproach, his great distress was triggered as he held the book and noticed a large wormhole through the poem *Jenny*, about a night with a prostitute. He had asked for the exhumation to be kept secret; however, plagued by conscience, he let some of his friends know and inevitably the news leaked out. In more destructive moments, perhaps he reflected on the thought that posterity would remember him more for his ghoulish action than for his great works of art and poetry. And that might have been true, had his genius as a painter and poet not been recognised early by the art and literary worlds.

As it was, from that occasion on, Gabriel was a very disturbed man. In addition to his 'artistic temperament', the death of Lizzie left him reclusive and eventually isolated, and now he had to come to terms with the distaste of her exhumation. He had not organised it, nor was he present. Those who officiated at the disinterment assured him that Lizzie was still 'perfect', and that her hair was still its beautiful red–gold colour. It was patently untrue, given the rate of decomposition of a body in the ground for seven years, but the truth was a harsh reality that Howell and his associates spared Gabriel out of nicety.

Yet Gabriel's memories haunted him for the rest of his life. How often did he taunt himself by remembering back to 1854, when he and Lizzie – both young and in love – had stayed at 5 High Street, Hastings – the place where it all began? They had been so happy then, and it had been such a romantic time, full of shared interests, Lizzie's recovery, long walks, friends and healthy seaside air. Why – and how – had it all gone so tragically wrong?

Of course, the importance of the events that took place in Hastings in 1854 has been much written about, interpreted, understood and, in some cases, misinterpreted and misunderstood. But the details of the part that Hastings itself played as a venue for those events have never really been explored, and most certainly 5 High Street had never been looked at with such a critical historical, architectural and archaeological eye before its purchase by us in 1997. What other clues did Hastings have lurking in the town's records and what additional information could the house itself offer the story?

In order to answer these questions one must first understand how Rossetti and Siddal came to be together and the circumstances surrounding their relationship. Their backgrounds were quite different, Gabriel being the son of middle-class, educated parents and Lizzie being the daughter of a Sheffield cutler, and so it was serendipity that they met at all.

Born 12 May 1828, Gabriel Charles Dante Rossetti was a complex character with abundant creative abilities, huge literary knowledge and a magnetically attractive personality. He was an adolescent prodigy, a visionary and a romantic free spirit. He disliked discipline and was a young rebel. He was over-idealistic, indolent and at times promised things he did not produce. His youthful high spirits, practical jokes and

Portrait of the Rossetti Family, 1864. (L to R) Gabriel, Christina, Mrs Rossetti and William. Photo by Charles Lutwidge Dodgson, better known as Lewis Caroll, who himself visited Hastings (Private Collection/The Bridgeman Art Library)

general robustiousness provided a safety valve to a more serious, underlying nature that was introspective and tended towards depression later in his life.

Gabriel's father and mother were Gabriele Rossetti, an Italian political exile, and Frances Polidori, a half English, half Italian governess. They ensured that their four children were well educated. Maria Francesca (born 1827) was an able student and a good poet. Gabriel shared a love of art, poetry and literature with his younger brother William (born 1829), who was an excellent writer. And, lastly, Christina (born 1830) was to become one of Britain's most esteemed female poets. Their childhood was interesting, and great fun, as they followed their hobbies of reading, writing and drawing. Italian was spoken with their father and they listened to conversations with other Italian associates, in a house that was always full of visitors.

In 1841 Gabriel enrolled at Sass's drawing school and in 1845 he attended the Antique School of the Royal Academy. He was not comfortable there, however, since he was not a natural draftsman, and he left in 1848, when he attached himself to the artist Ford Madox Brown, whom he had admired since 1844. They became life-long friends. In 1848, after the Royal Academy Exhibition, he sought out William Holman Hunt, whose painting 'Eve of St. Agnes' had greatly impressed him. They shared lodgings with studio space for a while.

By this period British art had reached its nadir and had become stultified and non-progressive. The Royal Academy, that veritable bastion of art foundation and prestige, had maintained a rigid structure where students spent their first three years drawing casts of classical Greek and Roman sculpture, before progressing on to life drawing and eventually painting. As a consequence, the Academy had become the epitome of conventional chocolate-box Victorian art, which some students like Gabriel thought produced bland, inconsequential pictures and pretty poses of children and animals. It was a reformation waiting to happen.

At this time Gabriel met up with another young painter from the Academy School, the precocious John Everett Millais. Millais, like Rossetti, had broken away from the Royal Academy system and was focusing on his technique. Holman Hunt, Rossetti and Millais were all a year on either side of twenty, middle class, energetic and idealistic, and they had all left the Academy Schools with a genuine dissatisfaction about the current state of British art. They joined forces with four other like-minded young men: William Rossetti, who recorded everything; Thomas Woolner, a sculptor; James Collinson, an artist later engaged to Christina Rossetti; and Frederick Stephens, an artist and later a critic of great influence.

Together they formed a 'secret society', calling themselves the Pre-Raphaelite Brotherhood (PRB), and, led by Rossetti and inspired by Millais' technical brilliance and Hunt's drive and determination, they began to study nature in detail and reproduce it in intense colour. They revived the art of painting over a white background (*chiaroscuro*), mimicking the brilliance of early Renaissance artwork. And they used live models in imagined settings, specifically seeking out appropriate people. Friends and family were often commandeered to sit in the appropriate period costume.

During the time that these young men were seeking attention for their new ideas, the Industrial Revolution had taken a hold in Britain, continuing to change the way of life of many people, whilst polarising the distribution of wealth. Inevitably people voiced their fears and sought refuge in art, poetry, literature and architecture. A modern-day art consultant, Martin Scadgell, explains this by saying that 'Art, like treacle sponge, is a comfort thing'. When Rossetti and the PRB turned to the chivalrous tales of knights, to mystical tales of bewitching and the tales of unrequited love, they were offering their viewers an escape from the grim reality of

Sir John Everett Millais, 1st Bt, by William Holman Hunt. chalk, 1853 (© National Portrait Gallery, London)

William Holman Hunt, by Sir John Everett Millais, watercolour and pencil on paper, 1854 (© Ashmolean Museum, University of Oxford, UK/The Bridgeman Art Library)

industrialisation into the comfort of an enchanting, and enchanted, world. 'It was an escape from an age, and a means of converting it', wrote William Gaunt in his twentieth-century biography of Rossetti.

Despite ridicule from the art world when they exhibited, the young men's art, and talent, gradually came to be recognised. John Ruskin, the great art critic, who became Rossetti's patron, assisted in that recognition. The PRB was, of course, an early protest group, being exclusively male, white and middle class. Yet these men derived much of their inspiration from young women models, known to them as 'stunners'. And, indeed, it was in this way that Elizabeth Siddal, known as Lizzie, came to be involved with their circle, having been discovered by the artists. Access to women like Lizzie was easy, since no chaperoning was necessary, and this made these working-class girls more appealing as models than their upper- and middle-class counterparts. These young women enjoyed much more freedom and inevitably this led to the cause of much trouble later on, as is discussed later in the book.

1850 was the year that changed Lizzie's life completely, taking her into a world as far removed from her own as she could have imagined. Little is known of Lizzie's early years. She was born Siddall, with two ls, but Gabriel Rossetti persuaded her to drop an l, because he felt it was more sophisticated. There remain gaps of many years where there is no information about her. No one sought out her family after her death, despite her mother living to be 92, to find those early details, or indeed to put her side of the story. It could have been something to do with their differences in class. Perhaps the Rossetti family tried to suppress any discussions concerning Gabriel's marriage to Lizzie, one which they certainly considered to be out of their class.

Lizzie was the daughter of Charles Siddall, a cutler, a working-class, skilled artisan fashioning, repairing and selling cutlery. Lizzie's father had moved from Sheffield to London, where he met and married Elizabeth Elenor Evans, a Londoner, in 1824. Ann was born in 1825, followed by Charles in 1827. Elizabeth Eleanor arrived on 25 July 1829 and was named after her mother, although an 'a' was added to her second name. Lydia came in 1831, Mary in 1833, Clara in 1836 and Henry in 1842. The children were born variously in Southwark, Bermondsey and Blackfriars, as father Charles extended his business opportunities.

There is little information about Lizzie's childhood or schooling. She was certainly literate and apparently enjoyed poetry, which she later started writing herself. She showed a flare for this and sensitivity for the written word. Her handwriting was clear and the tone of her letters was courteous and showed knowledge of the etiquette of the day. Some of her letters from 5 High Street, Hastings, still survive, as do Gabriel's.

Whilst working-class male children were generally destined to follow in their father's footsteps, opportunities for girls from the 'lower order' were limited, the favourite choices being dress-making, domestic service, laundering and lodging-house keeping. Given Lizzie's frailty and poor health, the three latter occupations would perhaps have been too physical for her. Whatever the reason, Lizzie became a milliner's assistant.

In 1850, Lizzie was working at Mrs Tozer's millinery shop in Cranbourne Alley, a slightly seedy area near Leicester Square. She was expected to work long hours for little return – often twelve-hour days, six days a week for as little as nine shillings. Holidays with pay did not exist for her class.

Generally, millinery was a thriving business as people sought to keep abreast of the latest fashions, but there were often slack periods. Since not many people went bareheaded then, milliners made a variety of headware – bonnets, hats, hoods, cloaks and accessories such as gloves and scarves, using a wide variety of materials.

This said, milliners' assistants were expected to dress well and behave genteelly towards their clientele. Respectability was an extremely important social advantage to

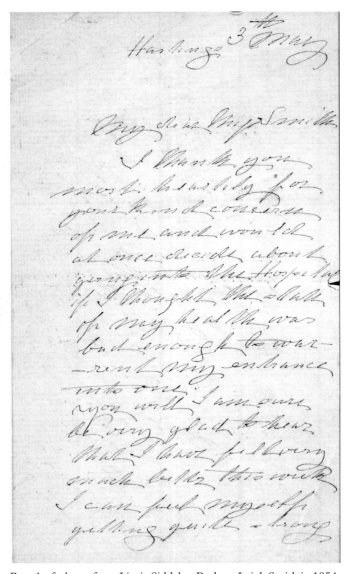

Page 1 of a letter from Lizzie Siddal to Barbara Leigh Smith in 1854
from 5 High Street (Janet Camp Troxell Collection. Manuscripts
Division, Department of Rare Books and Special Collections,
Princeton University Library)

the Victorians and was held to be an intrinsic value. Milliners also needed to have an
eye for colour and design, and to be able to copy the latest fashions, especially those
from France. Above all, they needed to be very skilled with a needle. We know from
her later artwork and ability to design and make her own dresses that Lizzie possessed
these creative attributes.

Page 2 of a letter from Lizzie Siddal to Barbara Leigh Smith in 1854
from 5 High Street (Janet Camp Troxell Collection. Manuscripts
Division, Department of Rare Books and Special Collections,
Princeton University Library)

It seems that Lizzie kept herself to herself whilst working at Mrs Tozer's, unlike many of the other female assistants, who were often flirtatious. As she interacted with her gentrified and better-off clientele, she would have observed and learned their behaviours and adopted some of them. It appeared that Lizzie was quite ladylike in her manners.

Lizzie was very striking in her appearance; tallish at 5 ft 7 in, with a mass of shining copper locks, deep-set, heavily lidded eyes, a largish nose and a slightly prominent lower lip. Her admirers seemed instantly enchanted by her beauty, which was described as like that of a medieval painting, although there were others who wondered what all the fuss was about and considered her not particularly beautiful. Yet those artistic young men whom Lizzie was about to meet saw her as stunning, and used her arresting appearance in a way that would impact on her life forever.

The favourite and most recounted story of Lizzie's discovery in 1850 tells of a young artist, Walter Deverell, who had been searching for a red-haired girl to model as Viola in his painting of *Twelfth Night*. On the recommendation of William Allingham, he went to Cranbourne Alley to check out the girls there. Then he spotted Lizzie. He was so immediately taken with her, and with her rightness as a model for *Twelfth Night*, that he knew he had to persuade her to sit for him. Both etiquette and common sense prevented him from bursting into Mrs Tozer's and putting the suggestion directly to Lizzie. Instead, he coerced his mother into going with him and used her maternal presence and air of respectability to influence Lizzie. Whatever was said, Lizzie was convinced, and this was probably reinforced by the thought of earning a shilling an hour for modelling. Set against her nine shillings a week as a milliner's assistant, modelling seemed to offer an attractive proposition.

Lizzie sat for Deverell unchaperoned while he worked on his version of Viola. Deverell was wildly enthusiastic about Lizzie's suitability, and was soon regaling his friends with details of her looks and suggesting that they should come and see for themselves.

Promptly, Gabriel Rossetti visited Deverell and met Lizzie. Instantly the die was cast. He set eyes on Lizzie and knew, in his own words, that 'his destiny was defined'. He began by making excuses to see her, brought her small gifts and treated her with gentlemanly courtesy. He at 20 years old and she at 19 were two young people drawn together in a drama that has been retold throughout history.

Gabriel had followed in his father's footsteps with his interest in the work of medieval poet Dante Alighieri and had, at seventeen, set about translating many of the verses. Dante wrote of his love for Beatrice and her absolute purity, and through his poetry he worshipped her. When Gabriel met Lizzie, his head was filled with these same notions, and Lizzie became his Beatrice. Unknown to either of them at this stage, Gabriel set up Lizzie to become the impossible – an idealisation. She was the answer to his dream, the focus of all his romantic ideals, his re-enactment of Dante's fanciful concept of Beatrice. Gabriel was probably not yet in touch with the sexual side of himself and only knew that he was in love with love in its purest form.

HASTINGS FROM THE EAST HILL
Published by Geo Wooll Printseller High St Hastings Nov. 1823

Hastings as Lizzie and Gabriel would have seen it; George Wooll lithograph (personal collection of J. Ridd & P. Marsden)

When Lizzie entered his life, Gabriel not only wooed her, but also courted his idealisation of her as the perfect woman. Lizzie was bound to fail in this, simply because she was human, and sooner or later was sure to fall from grace.

Lizzie Siddal suddenly found herself the equivalent of a supermodel today, a chic heroine who was not classically beautiful, but whose looks would translate well on to canvas. When Walter Deverell discovered her, he wrote in great excitement to William Holman Hunt:

> What a stupendously beautiful creature I have found. By Jove! She's like a queen, magnificently tall, with a lovely figure, a stately neck, and a face of the most finished and delicate modelling; the flow of surface from the temples over the cheek is exactly like the carving of a Pheidean goddess . . . and her hair is like dazzling copper and shimmers with lustre as she waves it down.

A star was born. In his imagination Deverell was already seeing her not only as a model, but also as his work of art, and she quickly became so to other members of

Hastings seafront from a George Wooll lithograph (personal collection of J. Ridd & P. Marsden)

the PRB. By 1851 she was sitting for Deverell, Hunt, Millais, Madox Brown and Rossetti. It is said that her best likeness was by Millais in his famous 'Ophelia'. The oft-repeated story is that in 1852 Millais acquired an old lacy dress and required Lizzie to pose in it by lying in a bath of water. He attempted to keep the water warm by placing lamps under the bath, but he became so absorbed that he did not notice when they went out. The water became cold and Lizzie caught a severe chill, at which point her father threatened Millais with an action for £50. However, the extra money Lizzie was making was useful at home, so Mr Siddall did not follow through, especially since Millais paid the doctor's bill.

How Lizzie was affected initially by her meteoric rise to leading-model status is not recorded, nor the effect of suddenly becoming the central focus of a group of somewhat bohemian young men. She was later said to have wondered whether anyone cared for her soul or whether everyone saw her as just a beautiful model with interesting hair. It was a cry from the heart of this young woman, who at such a tender age had been thrust into a world that was utterly alien to her, but that was seductive and intriguing, as well as a complete departure from her own.

Initially, perhaps she felt complimented by all the attention, and certainly the family welcomed her new earning potential, even if they felt ambivalent towards their daughter's questionable way of earning a living. But no one could have foreseen the effect that modelling was to have on Lizzie's life later on. What began for Lizzie as a romantic venture into the new and exciting world of art and artists eventually became a living nightmare, and at the centre of that story was one man – Dante Gabriel Rossetti.

When Gabriel met Lizzie, he was instantly enchanted by her looks, her beauty, her hair and her appropriateness as his model. She was his Beatrice incarnate and he, of all the PRB, began to pay her the most attention. For Lizzie it was a point of no return – there could be no turning back. She had compromised herself and her reputation by becoming a model, yet she was on the brink of the most exciting time of her life. This ingénue was worshipped by the men around her, singled out by the most charismatic and attractive man of all, given the opportunity to learn about art, poetry and literature, and offered the chance generally to broaden her horizons. Little wonder then that she allowed herself to be absorbed into the Pre-Raphaelite culture, enticed by its novelty, its vivacity and its dissimilarity to anything familiar to her.

By the time Millais was painting Lizzie as Ophelia, he noted that Gabriel was already in love with her, enticed by her 'unworldly simplicity and purity of aspect'.

By 1853 Gabriel and Lizzie appeared to be an item. He worshipped her as she modelled for him. He drew her again and again. Their snug existence at his rooms in Chatham Place was a two-way agreement, for Lizzie had begun to draw and paint, Gabriel teaching her the fundamentals of both watercolour and oil painting. Her figures were flat and perfectly Pre-Raphaelite, with good colours yet awkward poses, for Lizzie had no experience of life drawing. They lacked draftsmanship, hardly surprising since her teacher was poor at it himself. Gabriel was delighted with his pupil and she with her teacher. As the romance blossomed, a didactic and reverential relationship became an integral part of the seclusion.

Lizzie took to writing poetry too, morbid rhymes that were all about loss and death. These were very much in vogue at the time. Possibly Lizzie was mulling over her own mortality. Had she lived, who knows what treasures she may have written? Although never comparable with that of Christina Rossetti, Lizzie's poetry had tremendous emotional power and was intensely melancholic.

By this time Gabriel had asked Lizzie to give up work as a milliner and in so doing she was beholden to him for her welfare. Gabriel, through his utter obsession with her, was offering her protection. He also saw that she was unwell and struggling with her health. Gabriel himself, however, had no specific earning power at this time. While he produced little work – and that was watercolour – his PRB colleagues surged ahead.

3

Why Hastings?

Lizzie's health had always been poor, and her problems were cyclical in that she was ill on and off every few weeks. Gabriel, although not a natural sick-nurse, was compassionate and came to her aid when necessary. Was this the start of her learning that bouts of sickness reclaimed his attention quickly if it wandered?

History has muffled the voice of Lizzie Siddal. Many have recorded the events that surrounded her life in early 1854, but none is able to report what Lizzie herself thought or felt about her circumstances. Violet Hunt, Lizzie's biographer in 1932, described it as 'a voice behind glass or under water'. Lizzie's story was largely destroyed when Gabriel got rid of all her letters and effects on her death, as well as many drawings of her, and William Rossetti further reduced the evidence when he pruned Gabriel's letters on his death.

That Lizzie was ill, there was no question. However, scholars have differed in their opinions as to what was wrong with her. William Rossetti perhaps gave a clue as to what doctors thought her illness was in his description of her as 'tall, finely formed, with a lofty neck, greenish-blue unsparkling eyes, large perfect eyelids, brilliant complexion, and a lavish wealth of coppery gold hair'. The fact that her eyes were unsparkling and her complexion brilliant may have suggested to that she was tubercular, or consumptive. One of the main influences of tuberculosis on general health was 'a great malaise – an indefinite feeling of tiredness lasting for months. Sometimes it appears only as undue tiredness at the end of a day's work . . . It is partly physical and partly mental.' So said a medical book of the day. However, that would not account for Lizzie's continued vomiting, nor the absence of progressively tubercular lungs.

Throughout Lizzie's story there are conflicting accounts of what different doctors considered was wrong with her. A year after her visit to Hastings, she was sent by the art critic John Ruskin, who was interested in the work of both Gabriel and Lizzie, to Oxford to see Doctor Acland, a friend of Ruskin's. Acland did not think she was consumptive, but that her problem stemmed from 'mental power long pent up and overtaxed'. This could have been a typically Victorian male attitude that regarded women's constitutions as unsuitable for education or work. Perhaps it was a suggestion that Lizzie was suffering from stress – that of trying to become a self-supporting artist in a predominantly male world. This type of illness, related to body and mind, was little understood by the Victorians, but today would be described as psychological.

Trying to keep up with the dual lifestyle as milliner and model exhausted her. Her appetite was poor, she had stomach pains and she could not digest food, often vomiting what she ate. This combination of symptoms has caused modern day scholars to diagnose Lizzie's illness as an eating disorder called anorexia, which was an unrecognised condition in those days. For instance, in Cyclic Vomiting Syndrome (a rare form of anorexia in adults), attacks come on suddenly, induced by shock or fear, and, if prolonged, they engender feelings of weakness, powerlessness and defeat, and eventual depression. But this does not explain Lizzie's sudden recoveries, the immediate return of her energy that allowed her to walk about as though nothing had been wrong, nor the subsequent periods of wellness.

Perhaps Lizzie was anxious about her new role as model to the PRB and she felt pressure to eat little and keep her graceful figure. Lizzie's attacks seemed to have been triggered by situations beyond her control, when there was shock (Gabriel's infidelity), loss (a year without seeing Gabriel) or transition (her new world among artists and poets). Certainly her life changed dramatically as she spent time with Gabriel, for by this time she had mostly forfeited her previous world and was lost to it. She was in a most precarious position, because as yet Gabriel had not offered her marriage.

In 1854 Lizzie had been with Gabriel for two years and had known him for longer, believing that he would marry her and that all would be well. According to William Rossetti, who wrote 50 years later, he thought they had become engaged in 1852. There was no announcement, though, and no evidence exists that this ever happened.

It is likely that Lizzie remained celibate in order to remain chaste. It gave her a hold over Gabriel all the while he was in love with her and meant that she would never have to deal with an unwanted pregnancy. Meanwhile, Gabriel, for all his notions of romance, was now at a stage where his sexuality had been awakened and he was acutely aware of it. Even Gabriel realised that his life could not parallel his hero Dante's in not defiling Beatrice. He was ready for something to happen.

In January 1854, an event occurred that threatened Lizzie's unique position with Gabriel and triggered a long spell of ill health. Holman Hunt had become involved with his model Annie Miller, a barmaid, and was paying for her to be educated. He went to Palestine to paint, leaving Annie in the care of his friends. Before long, Gabriel was taking Annie out dancing and drinking, and eventually to bed.

Poor Lizzie! Whether she knew of Gabriel's betrayal or not, she certainly recognised Annie as a threat and was jealous of her. If she now gave in to Gabriel's sexual desires, she compromised herself, yet, if she held out longer, she risked losing him. It was a double bind and caused a highly stressful situation. As Lizzie agonised, her health went into decline. Whatever her illness, stress like this exacerbated it.

By about 1854, three young women in Gabriel's circle entered Lizzie's life and took a growing interest in her. They were Barbara Leigh Smith, Bessie Parkes and Anna Mary Howitt and, coincidentally, all three had connections with Hastings.

Barbara Leigh Smith divided her time between Hastings and London. She was a spirited watercolour landscape artist, who sought to further the cause of the women of her day. She was the daughter of a political reformer and MP, Ben Smith, who never married her mother Anne Longden, despite her bearing him five children. Anne was the daughter of a corn miller and it was undoubtedly this status that had inured Barbara to life, strengthened her resolve and gave her empathy towards women. She must have instantly summed up Lizzie's situation when she met her, and perhaps saw a parallel with her own mother, who had also once been a milliner.

Barbara's relatives considered her family 'tabooed' and her aspiring first cousin, Florence Nightingale, did not associate with her. Undeterred, Barbara became the leader of the 'Langham Place Set', the heartbeat of Victorian feminism. She campaigned tirelessly for women's rights in property, work and education, and she can be traced in Hastings in the early 1880s, often visiting the local suffragette group to offer encouragement. She was also a journalist and her first article had appeared in the *Hastings and St Leonards News* in 1848. Barbara continually befriended and helped poor women, eventually setting up a high school for girls and becoming co-founder of Girton College for women, Cambridge.

Barbara exhibited paintings of the Sussex area; many of these were of Hastings, such as 'The Sea, Hastings', 'Sunrise, Hastings', 'After Sunset; Hastings', 'Sea at Hastings' and 'Sunset After Storm, Bexhill'. A sketch book of hers, now in the Girton College archive, shows her delightful drawings of the seafront at Hastings.

Barbara's constant friend and companion was journalist Bessie Rayner Parkes, who edited the feminist magazine *The English Woman's Journal*. Bessie's and Barbara's families had some similarities – both non-conformists, both involved in political reform, both radical in attitude and both having houses in Hastings – in fact almost next door to each other in the fashionable Pelham Crescent, along the main promenade.

The two women discussed everything during their lifelong friendship, although

Barbara Leigh Smith Bodichon in 1857 (by 'Holmes of New York', ambrotype; © National Portrait Gallery, London)

Bessie Raynor Parkes (watercolour by an unknown artist; © The Mistress and Fellows, Girton College, Cambridge)

there was a blip when Bessie turned Catholic in 1864. Bessie was less charismatic than Barbara, but equally dogged in her pursuit of a better quality of life for women.

Bessie was attracted to the 'free wild spirits the Smiths always seemed to have' and wrote on one journey south:

> To Hastings; mad in the train, singing, shouting, yelling, laughing. Oh how happy I was, thinking of the glorious winter to come, to read, all the lovely rides, all the reading and the talk with Barbara, all the acting and the music, and the seaweeds and the ferns; Ecclesbourne, Fairlight and all the jolly places.

Bessie was devoted to Barbara, so much so that in the 1932 book by Violet Hunt entitled *The Wife of Rossetti* she is described as 'Bessie the Brick'. Bessie eventually married a Frenchman, Louis Belloc, and had two children, the well-known poet Hillaire Belloc and an equally literary daughter Mary Lowndes, who later wrote her mother's biography. Bessie was to play a very active part in Lizzie Siddal's visit to Hastings.

The third member of this literary trio was Anna Mary Howitt. She was also a lifelong friend of Barbara's. Their families met initially in Hastings in 1845, one of a trusted set of friends in the town who were not offended by the family's irregular social status.

'Shipping off the Coast Hastings' by Barbara Leigh Smith (© Hastings Museum)

The Howitts accepted the Leigh Smiths and enjoyed their company. Both parents were writers and, through them, both Bessie and Barbara were introduced into literary circles. Mrs Howitt is perhaps best known for those familiar lines '"Will you walk into my parlour?" said the spider to the fly'. Her daughter Anna Mary was attending Sass's school of art in London at the same time as Gabriel Rossetti and, although unable to continue because of financial hardship, Anna Mary continued to paint. She, in turn, introduced Barbara Leigh Smith to other women artists and so the circle was complete. The Howitts often visited Hastings and lodged at Clive Vale Farm, near the village of Ore on the outskirts of the town.

Once Gabriel had introduced Lizzie into Barbara's circle, these three women made a real attempt to get to know her. Initially they were interested in Lizzie because they enjoyed Gabriel's company. Bessie declared at one time, 'Dante is my favourite of these young men', meaning the PRB. The fascination was perhaps greater because they knew of Lizzie's modest beginnings and knew that she had been his model and pupil before she had become his love. Barbara also saw her as an aspiring artist. 'She is a genius and will . . . be a great artist, her gift discovered by a strange accident such as rarely befalls women', she wrote to Bessie. Lizzie had just submitted a drawing entitled 'Pippa Passes' to the newly formed Folio Society, where her work was displayed alongside Barbara's, Anna Mary's and Gabriel's.

As Lizzie became more exhausted, so her health went into decline. When Gabriel introduced her to his circle of friends, what they saw – and were immediately concerned about – was a sick woman who they thought might be dying.

The temptation to offer a helping hand was just too great for as generous spirit as Barbara's. She undoubtedly saw Lizzie as a woman whom she could help by encouraging her to develop her talents, but at that moment Lizzie was very ill and needed practical help. Barbara was convinced that Lizzie was dying, and wrote to Bessie in a letter from Hastings: 'I still believe she is going fast.'

One can imagine the scene – the three friends Barbara, Bessie and Anna Mary meeting up at the Howitt's London home, The Hermitage, and discussing Gabriel's new love. Curiosity would have got the better of them, especially as Gabriel had confided in Barbara about Lizzie. 'Dante R told me all about her', she wrote to Bessie. It was Barbara who suggested to Lizzie that she should go into Florence Nightingale's 'Home For the Care of Gentlewomen' in Harley Street, London. Lizzie quickly declined, however, probably nervous about being confined anywhere, especially amongst the well off, where her freedom of seeing Gabriel alone would be curtailed.

It was at this point that Anna Mary, or maybe her mother, suggested that Lizzie should see Dr Wilkinson, their homeopathic doctor, and they probably arranged the appointment and paid for it.

Violet Hunt in *The Wife of Rossetti* makes reference to Dr Wilkinson. Her book about Lizzie, published in 1932, was her last book, but her first biography. Her style is flowery and seemingly full of tittle-tattle, which has caused most scholars to dismiss the book as an unreliable account. One scholar has suggested that her rambling style was the result of her being in the third stage of syphilis, known then as 'General Paralysis of the Insane', and that her intellect was failing because of it.

However, whilst I am unable to comment on the veracity of the rest of her book, I can attest that, from my research and experience of Hastings, Violet's details of the town, and of 5 High Street, are accurate in almost every aspect, as I will describe later. I feel therefore, that her description of Lizzie's appointment with Dr Wilkinson is also likely to be correct.

Violet suggested that Dr Wilkinson, the Howitts' homeopath, had summed up Lizzie as consumptive: 'Long legs, long fingers, long throat, dullish prominent eyes, luxuriant hair – all characteristic of one type of what we now colloquially call T.B. Distinct curvature of the spine!' It was not true, as we now know. Apparently Lizzie complained to him of the cold and damp of her home, and the stench of London. Her comments were justified, for the Thames was an open sewer for the excrement of three million people and yet was still used for drinking water, rendering London rife with disease, sickness and epidemics of cholera and typhoid. There were fogs, smogs and evil gases, outpouring from the industries and from half a million coal fires. Horse droppings littered the streets. This is why London became the perfect target for Charles Dickens in his hard-hitting novels of the time. He referred to London as 'the great and dirty city'.

Violet Hunt wrote that the outcome of the appointment with Dr Wilkinson was that he recommended Lizzie to see Dr Hale, a homeopathic doctor in Hastings. When I checked, I found records for the latter in Hastings. Robert Douglas Hale was born in Dublin but trained as an MD at St Andrews. He lived with his wife Tedlie, a Parisian, his sons Charles Edward and Arthur and his daughters Mary and Florence at 26 Grand Parade, St Leonards on Sea, where he had a fashionable practice. Because of the Howitts' familiarity with both homeopathy and with Hastings, it is probable that they knew Dr Hale. Or perhaps Barbara, with her greater knowledge of Hastings, may have seen his advertisement in the local newspaper, the *Hastings and St Leonards Gazette*. He had recently opened a homeopathic dispensary on 17 December 1853 at 8 High Street. Maybe it was the dispensary's proximity to 5 High Street that made the young women feel that the lodgings would be a convenient for Lizzie. At any rate, the outcome decided; 'Miss Siddal was to be rushed off to Hastings' for a period of recuperation.

Barbara, unable to resist, wrote to Bessie sometime between 9 and 13 April in Hastings with the news: 'Private now my dear ... A secret then and you are to help. She Miss Siddal is going down to Hastings on Saturday . . .'. Barbara was alerting her friend that she was to be involved in helping to find appropriate lodgings in Hastings for Lizzie. Presumably Gabriel helped out, although he was always short of money. Possibly Violet Hunt's account was right and that he borrowed a sum from his Aunt Charlotte, his mother's sister, and from his poet friend William Allingham, who had Lizzie's welfare at heart.

So, whilst Gabriel had his mind full of other things – his father ill and John Ruskin offering patronage – Lizzie found her excursion to Hastings had been organised for her. Her well-meaning friends, and a homeopathic doctor's recommendation, meant that she was returning to the seaside resort again. She had been there to recuperate in August 1852, some time after the 'Ophelia' episode.

In 1823 an entrepreneurial young man called George Wooll moved into 5 High Street, Hastings, and set up a 'Repository of Arts' in the two front rooms. His talents were diverse and included drawing, printing, writing and publishing, as well as shop keeping. He wrote two guidebooks, the second being *Wooll's Strangers' Guide to Hastings and St. Leonards*, published from 5 High Street in 1833–34. Although this was 20 years before Lizzie and Gabriel visited, Wooll's guide would still have been pertinent to them, for it described eloquently the good life to be had in Hastings for the tourist.

It is interesting to note that in describing the position of hotels and lodging houses, Wooll also mentions the benefits of each location. For instance: 'They who suffer from impaired digestion find a free air with sufficient warmth in The Square, The Croft, . . .'. He continues, 'The consumptive invalid meets the requisite warmth and shelter in High Street, All Saints Street, . . . Pelham Crescent,' and so on. Once Dr Wilkinson had suggested that Lizzie was consumptive, maybe Barbara Leigh Smith and Bessie Parkes used their knowledge of Hastings Old Town to find just the right location for her. Coupled with the fact that she needed something reasonably priced, then 5 High Street was ideal, although there had been some inflation since Wooll's time, when 'a good sitting room and sleeping room may be had for a guinea'.

At the end of the eighteenth century the Napoleonic wars and subsequent naval blockades had made holidaying on the Continent impossible, so alternative British watering places were sought. Suddenly Britain's coast was discovered, and found to be delightful; wealthy invalids and society figures hastened to Hastings to be cured and to be seen.

Previously a tiny fishing town, Hastings became a resort second only to Brighton in reputation. It had followed Brighton's lead and had gentrified itself. Before seaside resorts, there were inland spa towns in places such as Bath, Hotwells in Bristol and Tunbridge Wells, but gradually the fashion changed from making a journey from town to town to travelling from coastal resort to coastal resort.

The accoutrements of the hydrotherapy spa towns were replicated, using seawater instead of spring water. The latest bathing machines and water-dipping paraphernalia were installed for those seeking a cure. Gradually other health and social requirements appeared for the 'dedicated followers of fashion'. Visitors wanted beautiful scenery, excellent shopping, social events, reading rooms and libraries, bookshops, coffee houses and clubs and societies of interest. Following the sick, the wounded and the weary were the doctors who supervised them, and who became wealthy in the process. Possibly Lizzie's Dr. Hale was one such medic. Brighton led the way, but Hastings was close behind.

Alongside this wealthy image, Hastings had its darker side. Almost all the residents

Drawn by Paul Fischer,

FISH MARKET, HASTINGS.
Pub. by G.Wooll, Printseller, 5 High Street, Hastings.

& on Stone by G.Rowe.

The Old Hastings Fish Market c. 1824, George Wooll (Personal Collection of J.Ridd & P. Marsden)

were involved in smuggling until the 1830s, and these activities supplemented the earnings of the poorer people, whilst allowing others to become very wealthy. There is no doubt that 5 High Street was rebuilt in about 1797 on the proceeds of smuggling. Mary Wenham's brother-in-law was an extremely wealthy man and he helped the widow by building her a new house where she could take in lodgers and so earn her own keep.

The fishermen were generally poverty-stricken, but by the time of Lizzie's visit they had found plenty of opportunities for bolstering their meagre incomes. They had whelk, oyster and cockle stalls, they picked hops, sold flowers, offered boat rides, made shell ornaments and, of course, sold their catches of fish at the 'Dutch Auction' on the beach. George Wooll explained:

> The boatman puts up all he has got for a good price. If none offer, he says something less, and gradually comes down ere he gets an offer. The first that does gets the lot.

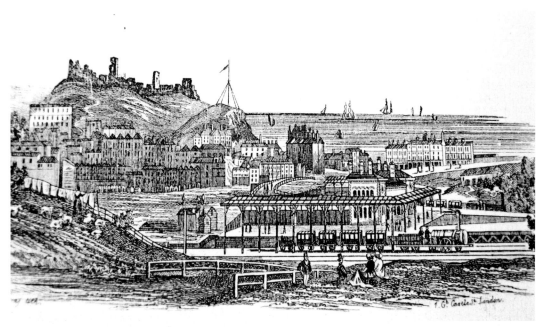

Print of Hastings Railway Station c.1850 (Hastings Museum and Art Gallery)

A big local trade was fish smoking, done in fish-drying houses called 'deezes'. A previous occupant of No. 5, Mary Sargeant, née Moore, owned a deeze along the seafront. When smoked, herrings became 'red herrings'.

By 1848 the railway had made travelling to Hastings much easier than by stagecoach or sea. The new railway station opened in 1851, and so was only three years old when Lizzie and Gabriel saw it. So, also, was born the 'day tripper'. Londoners came in abundance and the small town in the valley extended westwards. Large terraces of grand Victorian properties were built and the population swelled. People cashed in, selling off plots of land behind their houses for infill buildings, and this gave rise to the tightly-packed configuration of the Old Town as we see it today.

In 1828 the town of St Leonards began to be built, started by James Burton, with later additions from his tenth son, Decimus. This purpose-built seaside resort was a new phenomenon, designed by the top architects of the day, and was an instant hit with visitors. It was classy and fashionable, and was an excellent place to recuperate if one was ill, which was why Dr Hale chose it for his practice.

Since the mid eighteenth century Hastings had been a magnet for artists and poets, who loved the spectacular scenery, the verdant vegetation and the gentle coastal walks. When Hastings deliberately chose to offer a similar lifestyle to the inland spa towns,

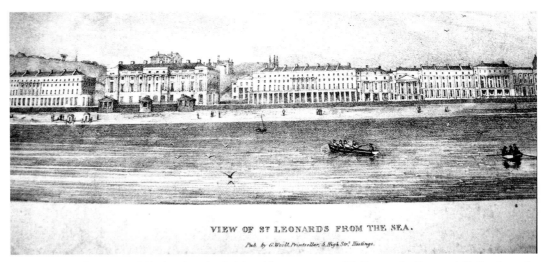

George Wooll print c. 1830 showing the fashionable new town of St Leonards (Personal Collection of J. Ridd & P. Marsden)

numbers of eminent personalities visited, including the poets Byron, Keats, Lamb and Hood and the artists Joseph Farington, Edward Dayes and Thomas Girton.

Gabriel and his family had always been aware of Hastings. In 1843, prior to the railway being built, the Rossetti parents had lodged at 9 High Street, four doors from No. 5, and so could recommend the area. Gabriele Rossetti had been trying to shake off a particularly virulent bout of bronchitis.

In August 1852, Gabriel was writing to his sister Christina, 'I shall very possibly be going to Hastings for a few days'. His intention was to join Lizzie, who was recuperating from illness, possibly connected with her experience of the prolonged cold bath when modelling for Millais's Ophelia. There are no details of Lizzie's visit, but there is a clue in that, when considering her visit in 1854, Lizzie already knew Hastings, and therefore probably felt more comfortable about returning to somewhere that was familiar. There are no further details as to whether Gabriel went to see her.

Also in August 1852, William Holman Hunt, William Rossetti, Edward Lear and John Everett Millais all visited Hastings, Hunt and Lear for a prolonged visit in order to paint. It seems likely that, had Gabriel arrived in town whilst they were all there, the young men would have arranged to meet up. No one records such a meeting, and so perhaps we can assume that Gabriel never made it, or that the dates of the respective visits did not coincide conveniently.

'William Rossetti having a week's vacation agreed to come with me, and we went down together', wrote William Holman Hunt of their visit to Hastings in August 1852. They met up with Robert Martineau, a former lawyer turned artist, whose family owned Fairlight Lodge, a large house on the edge of the village of Fairlight, to the east of Hastings. William Holman Hunt had agreed to take on Robert as a student. In turn, Martineau introduced Holman Hunt to Edward Lear, the lyricist and painter.

Lear, of course, is better known for his nonsense poems, limericks and 'bosh', but he was a very fine painter also, and had been seeking Holman Hunt's advice about painting. They met Lady Waldegrave, the owner of 5 High Street. 'I was disgusted at being apriently [sic] so rude to Lady Waldegrave', Lear wrote, after he had refused to sing to her in case he 'made a noise like a dyspeptic mouse in a fit'. In 1852–1853, he took lodgings at Hastings Lodge, home of MP Frederick North, where he encouraged daughter Marianne in botanic painting. Marianne North's now famous gallery in Kew Gardens was renovated a few years ago. Her father, Frederick North, was Mayor of Hastings during Lizzie and Gabriel's visit.

Lear was so enthused by Hunt's suggestion of painting from nature that he invited himself down. He arranged rooms for himself and the two Williams at Clive Vale Farm close by, which was also a retreat for the Howitt family and had probably been recommended by them.

'Whilst the singer of nonsense rhymes and I were busy working, a letter from Millais announced that he would come down on Saturday night and spend Sunday with us', wrote Hunt. The young men were very impressed with the beautiful green, undulating countryside, and spent much of their time outdoors walking and painting. Hunt painted 'Our English Coasts' ('Strayed Sheep'), and two years later Millais returned and to paint 'L'Enfant du Regiment' and 'The Blind Girl'.

Christina Rossetti's name is to poetry what her brother's is to art. Revered in her own lifetime, she is still esteemed as one of the leading women poets of all time. To Christina, too, Hastings was a special place, and her links with the town were closer than any of the other Rossettis, because she stayed longer, although no blue plaques mark her visits to the seaside resort. She had a prolonged stay at 81 High Street, on the opposite side and further down from 5 High Street. Her life was tinged with ill health and protracted recoveries, for which her solution was to seek refuge in coastal watering places. Consequently, she never worked.

Her visits to Hastings were long after Gabriel's and Lizzie's. In 1864 she was recovering from illness and was enchanted with the town; she later wrote it into a long story called the *The Waves of this Troublesome World: A Tale Of Hastings Ten Years Ago*, published in 1870. In it she wrote:

Perhaps there is no pleasanter watering place in England . . . than Hastings and the Sussex coast . . . .. The old town, nestling in a long narrow valley, flanked by

Drawn by G. Row.

HASTINGS CASTLE *from near the* HOP GARDENS,
Pub. by G. Wooll, Printseller, 5, High Str. Hastings.

Hastings was surrounded by stunning scenery, as shown in this George Wooll Print, c. 1825 (Personal Collection of J. Ridd & P. Marsden)

the East and West hills, looks down upon the sea. At the valley mouth, on the shiningly beach, stands the fishmarket, where boatmen disembark the fruit of daily toil; where traffic is briskly plied, and maybe haggling rages; where the bare-legged children dodge in and out between the stalls; where now and then a travelling show – dwarf, giant, or whatnot – arrests for brief days its wanderings.

This same description of Hastings would have applied in 1854 when Lizzie and Gabriel visited ten years earlier. Although that fish market has been replaced today by a more modern version nearby, fish is still sold from the beach and Hastings boasts one of the remaining beach-launching fishing fleets left in Britain today and the largest in Europe.

In April 1873 Christina and her mother returned to Hastings with a consumptive cousin, and she came again in 1884, during which time she visited the grave of her one-time fiancé, Charles Bagot Cayley. Despite the broken romance, they had remained friends. Christina went quietly to Hastings Borough Cemetery, the huge swathe of land that had still been up for tender in 1854 during Lizzie and Gabriel's visit.

Other artists who had connections with Hastings were J.M.W. Turner, Samuel Prout and in later Victorian times Whistler, whose mother lived there from 1875 till her death in 1881. She was buried in the same Borough Cemetery. All three artists visited several times, and painted on these occasions. Later Edward Burne Jones designed a stained glass window for St Mary Magdelene Church in St Leonards.

This existing strong association between the Rossettis and Hastings, coupled with Gabriel's friendship with Barbara and Bessie, ensured that the town was destined to become the stage on which the unfolding drama between Gabriel Rossetti and his red-haired 'stunner' Lizzie Siddal was to be played out. Lizzie came for the recuperative benefits of the seaside, yet at the same time she and Gabriel were part of the trend, keeping alive a long literary and artistic heritage. No small wonder, then, that Gabriel and Lizzie continued their art work during their stay and that his drawings from their modest lodgings at 5 High Street in the heart of Old Town Hastings have attracted world-wide attention from art historians.

4

Hastings – The Halcyon Days

Lizzie languished listlessly in the adjustable armchair, posing informally for Gabriel as he unwittingly provided 5 High Street with a most powerful and unrivalled legacy. His seven drawings of Lizzie at the house heralded the beginning of his obsession with this wistful and withdrawn creature, as he drew her again and again. Later, in London, it became noticeably habitual, causing his sister Christina to write a poem beginning:

> One face looks out from all his canvases,
> One selfsame figure sits or walks or leans:

In that upstairs room at 5 High Street, an entranced and besotted Gabriel drew Lizzie simply, and endearingly, portraying her frailty and vulnerability through a variety of positions, sometimes sitting or standing, sometimes reading or resting. He captured her very essence on paper and unknowingly provided art historians with a heritage of unparalleled quality. The drawings were some of Gabriel's finest, not for their technicality, but for the refinement and intensity engendered in them.

Not only did Gabriel depict Lizzie's soul, but he left vital clues about her hairstyle, dress and the furniture in her room at Number 5. Gabriel's perspective was often inaccurate, but these simple pencil drawings evoke a silent pathos, allowing the observer to glimpse the still depths within. They are also helpful in reconstructing the room in which they worked. Even today it is possible to see that there is only one room that it could possibly have been, because only one windowsill matches the drawing and allows for the right amount of furniture on either side. This was the front bedroom, opposite the visitor's parlour. It was the one that my husband and I used and, on either side of the window, I hung the two drawings of Lizzie posed by the windowsill, so that I could always imagine her there.

The drawings are unarguably the most important feature of the modest part that 5 High Street played in the story of Lizzie and Gabriel's visit to Hastings. Today they can be found in various art museums nationally and internationally, including the Victoria & Albert in London, the Ashmolean Museum in Oxford, the Fitzwilliam Museum in Cambridge, the Cecil Higgins Art Gallery in Bedford and the Birmingham

Museum and Art Gallery. John Ward, writer of the forward to Virginia Surtees's *Rossetti's Portraits of Elizabeth Siddal* declared: 'It is a unique series. There is nothing comparable in European art.'

The young couple's journey to Hastings was uneventful. On Saturday 22 April 1854, Lizzie and Gabriel left Blackfriars at about 12.30 p.m. and caught a horse-drawn cab to London Bridge Station. According to Violet Hunt, Lizzie travelled in pale lilac, with her red hair looped up in her own unique fashion. At the station they bought a return ticket for him, priced £1, and a single for her. Gabriel's intention was to go back to London once he had seen Lizzie settled. They caught the 1.30 p.m. train, which was due to arrive at 5.06 p.m. in Hastings, when Bessie Parkes would meet them. The journey seems excessively long, but the timetables of the day quote these

5 East Parade, overlooking the fisherman's beach, where Bessie Parkes stayed with her friend Emma Evers when greeting Gabriel and Lizzie on their arrival in Hastings (Past Historic Archive)

The Cutter Inn today (Past Historic Archive)

times and give a cost of £1 for a return ticket. The train went via Reigate, Tonbridge, Tunbridge Wells and Battle.

Bessie was staying with her friend Emma Evers at 5 East Parade, on the seafront a few doors from the Cutter Inn. Before she met them, Bessie had walked to Pelham Crescent in bright sunshine. On their arrival, Bessie, Lizzie and Gabriel probably took a cab from the station and went out along the seafront, where Lizzie would have smelled the wonderful freshness of the salt air and watched a lively sea, turned leaden grey under a by now cloudy sky.

As they came from the station, they passed through the Priory Valley, where once the original town of Hastings had stood. They saw the imposing family homes on Pelham Crescent, built in 1824 by architect Joseph Kaye, after blasting away the rock face of the cliffs and cutting a new road along the front. Little did Kaye or anyone

The medieval High Street of old Hastings up which Gabriel and Lizzie passed in order to reach Mrs Elphick's house at Number 5. The former bank, now the Old Bank House, is on the left (Past Historic Archive)

else realise that this blasting was to leave the Castle, built in 1068, in a severely weakened state.

Gabriel, Lizzie and Bessie journeyed along the seafront, Bessie probably pointing out the Cutter Inn, run by landlord William Payne, where Gabriel was to stay that night, and they turned left into High Street just past it. As they drove up Hastings' main thoroughfare, no doubt Lizzie would have been interested in the shops and businesses that were to surround her for the next few weeks. She would have noted the Savings Bank at the Town Hall; Robert Lyle's Drapery at Number 34; the Misses E.C. & K. Job's Milliner's and Dressmaker's at Number 30; Mrs G. Wheeler's Confectionery at Number 17 and perhaps Mrs Carpenter's, the straw bonnet maker's, at Number 104 on the high pavement. There were several fruiterers and greengrocers, boot- and shoemakers and retailers, an ironmonger's and Richard Page's Eating House at Number 29. They could not have known it, but W.J. Gant, at Number 10, had produced the first map of Hastings in about 1850 that detailed every house and showed the shape of every garden in High Street, including Number 5. This shape was unchanged when Lizzie and Gabriel saw it, and remained so until we altered it after having had the excavation there.

They arrived outside the very ordinary grey building that was 5 High Street. A photograph in Violet Hunt's book (circa 1932) shows 5 High Street as it was before the addition of mathematical tiles and weatherboarding, and it would have looked the same to Lizzie and Gabriel. Mrs Elphick, the landlady, would have swung open the door in answer to their knock and smiled her welcome to the three young people. Bessie would have greeted her former acquaintance warmly and introduced Gabriel and Lizzie. They stepped down into the dining hall with its net curtains for privacy, its warm brick fireplace clad in boards, with a range in front, and its flap shelf of telling medicine bottles – for Mr Elphick was an invalid. Mrs Elphick would eventually have introduced them to Miss A. Von Esch, a singing teacher, who was the only other lodger there, and to Sarah Veness, the servant.

It seems that these local people were well known to Barbara and Bessie, and they were pleased to offer them their best service. Not only did Mary Elphick make Lizzie welcome that day, but she found her a comfortable upstairs room at the front of the house, offered them tea and settled Lizzie whilst Bessie walked back down the road with Gabriel to show him his lodgings at the Cutter Inn just around the corner on the sea front.

The story of Gabriel and Lizzie coming to 5 High Street has been repeated in numerous biographies of them both and the name 'Mrs Elphick' is always mentioned in a rather distant and dismissive way, as though she were not quite germane to the

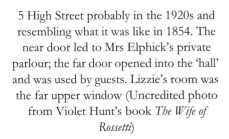

5 High Street probably in the 1920s and resembling what it was like in 1854. The near door led to Mrs Elphick's private parlour; the far door opened into the 'hall' and was used by guests. Lizzie's room was the far upper window (Uncredited photo from Violet Hunt's book *The Wife of Rossetti*)

story. However, the opposite is true. Lizzie and Gabriel fared well in Hastings, and Mrs Elphick's warmth and kindness was a central feature. So, who was this mysterious Mrs Elphick and what role did she play during the young people's stay at the lodging house?

Mary Elphick, formerly Mary Henley, was the daughter of Thomas and Mary Henley and was christened on 17 October 1790, at Brede, just outside Hastings. John Elphick, the son of John and Philadelphia Elphick, was baptised at St. Clement's Church, Hastings, on 2 June 1793. Presumably Mary and John met in Hastings, where he was a shipwright, and they were married by the Rector, Webster Whistler, on 28 June 1820 at All Saints Church, with John Mander and Sarah Henley, Mary's sister, witnessing their marriage.

The Reverend Webster Whistler was from a Battle family, where his descendants still live today. The Vicar was a vibrant character known to all in the small town. On one occasion the parson ran into a tradesman's shop crying:

'Well, I've done a most extraordinary thing this morning!' '
What's that?" asked the tradesman.
'Why,' said Whistler, 'I've tied a woman to a rock.'
'What made you do that?'
'Because she wanted me to,' quoth Whistler. 'You see, I've married her to a man
named Rock.'

The Whistlers were known smugglers in the Hastings area and there is a connection
with the artist Whistler.

The Elphicks were an old Hastings family with namesake relatives who were bakers
living in All Saints Street. By the time they were listed in the 1851 census, John was
58 and Mary was 60 and they were living on the seafront at 2 East Parade. Between
then and 1854 they had moved to 5 High Street with the intention of running it as a
lodging house, because John had become ill and presumably needed constant nursing.
Although he was recorded as the landlord in the town directory, it was obvious that
the move had been made because of his poor health and that running a lodging house
was a job Mary could quite easily take over. It afforded her the time to look after him
and an income to compensate for his loss of earnings as a shipbuilder.

In April 1854, when Bessie Parkes brought Lizzie and Gabriel to Number 5, it was
clear that both she and Barbara Leigh Smith knew both the Elphicks and their servant
Veness. In a letter to Bessie between 6 and 13 April 1854, whilst trying to organise
Lizzie's stay in Hastings, Barbara had written:

Will you dear see if the room Veness had by St. Clements Church is to let. If
not to let then will you ask Mrs Elphick where there is a room with <u>sun</u> and a
good woman and for a few shillings a week say 7 or 8s or less if possible. It
must be big enough to do for eating and drawing and sleeping.

Barbara's tone to Bessie suggests that they were both familiar with the Elphicks and
Veness, and this was so, for Sarah Veness had been a servant in the house at least
from the time of the 1851 census. Both Barbara and Bessie knew that because they
knew the Veness family (then pronounced Venus) – they were their neighbours.
Barbara, at 9 Pelham Crescent, was right next door to the Veness family at Number
10 and Bessie Parkes had been at 6 Pelham Crescent until 1853. George and Hannah
Veness had ten children, born between 1825 and 1844. They were Emma, Frances,
Ann, Sarah, George William, Elizabeth, Eliza, Matilda, Jane and Ellen – nine girls and
one boy. The first seven children were all baptised at All Saints and the last three at St

Letter from Barbara Leigh Smith to Bessie Parkes in 1854 asking her to set up Lizzie and Gabriel's stay in Hastings (© The Mistress and Fellows, Girton College, Cambridge)

Clement's, suggesting that perhaps the Veness family had lived in both parishes before their move westwards to the newer part of Hastings.

Sarah Veness was the fourth child and fourth daughter. While she worked at 5 High Street, her father worked as a carpenter in Post Office Passage a few yards down the High Street. Being the kindly and gregarious person she was, Barbara would have taken an interest in the children's progress over the years and it was perhaps through Sarah's position as a servant at 5 High Street that Barbara and Bessie got to know Mrs Elphick.

As well as Sarah Veness's name entering Rossetti/Siddal biographies worldwide, descendents of the Veness family have added interest to Hastings history. In 1886 John Veness was lost at sea when the fishing boat *John and Elizabeth* capsized. In 1888 Harry Veness hanged himself because of debt. In the 1970s, during alterations to 5 High Street, Marshall Coombes, the previous owner, found a note in a pickled onion jar underneath the fireplace of the dining hall saying, 'Veness, carpenter, did these refurbishments in 1952.' And in 1958 Harry Veness wrote his memories of Hastings

Pelham Crescent, overlooking the sea, the former home of Barbara Leigh Smith who helped organise the visit of Lizzie to Hastings in 1854 (Past Historic Archive)

in a book called *Whatever Happened to the Oojah Kappivy?* (meaning 'Thingummybob'), in which there is a section on a twentieth century resident of 5 High Street, Alexis Taggart. Harry's son Bruce continues to produces plays at the local Stables Theatre, formerly the stables of Countess Waldegrave, a previous owner of 5 High Street.

It is easy to believe that Mary Elphick was a caring, sympathetic person; after all, she was tending her sick husband. Undoubtedly, she saw at a glance the state of affairs between Lizzie and Gabriel – that they were very much in love and that Lizzie was unwell. Compassion for their situation may have led Mrs Elphick to offer Gabriel a room at Number 5 later.

Throughout the time Lizzie and Gabriel spent at Number 5, it is obvious that Mary Elphick facilitated the situation by allowing their relationship to grow. When the young people requested that they work together in Lizzie's room, Mary was comfortable with that. She was from the working class herself, and recognised that the Victorian convention of chaperoning was not necessary here.

Mary Elphick liked to gossip. She may have enjoyed telling the young couple stories about not one, but two, ghosts at Number 5. A former tenant, said Violet

The narrow passage leading from the top of the main stairs to the attic stairs, supposedly haunted by an old man. This was a dark passage with no window in 1854. Lizzie's bedroom is on the right, the guests' parlour is on the left (Past Historic Archive)

Hunt, a Mrs Stanforth, complained of the ghost in the attic – 'an old man whom no one ever saw but whose footsteps followed one upstairs'. Both Mrs Stanforth and her tenants were forced to leave, said Mrs Elphick, until she had enclosed the staircase in 'stoothing', a local word, meaning lath and plaster. Quite how Mrs Stanforth knew that the ghost was an old man if she never saw him is questionable, but it is a nice tale. Violet Hunt's details were not quite correct, as only a Mrs Stanfield could be found during research. 'Well then there was another', wrote Violet Hunt in Lizzie's biography. Apparently local people had christened the kitchen at Number 5 'The Corpse Hole', owing to the fact that it was haunted by a woman whose body had been laid out there before being thrown into the Bourne Stream at the bottom of the garden at night. She returned to haunt the occupants.

One might easily dismiss these as 'tall tales' except that a smuggling story exists so similar to this last one that it might be almost believable. A former owner of 5 High

Street, Jean Taylor, told me a corresponding story that she had heard from neighbours during the 1950s, but, instead of a woman, it was a male Customs Officer who had been captured and was given rough treatment.

No one seemed unduly bothered by the ghostly duo. It should be noted here for the faint at heart that, whilst there may have been ghosts then, no such phenomena exist today at 5 High Street!

Violet Hunt gave details of how Lizzie's doctor, Dr Hale at 8 High Street, visited Lizzie on her second day and how he suggested that Gabriel should become acquainted with Mr William Smith, the chemist in George Street. There was indeed a William Smith, chemist, druggist and mineral water manufacturer, at 20 George Street. Gabriel mentioned him in one of his letters home to his brother on 9 May: 'Mr and Mrs W. Smith have been most kind and attentive to her.' William, born in Penmore, Worcestershire, and Elizabeth, born in Bishops Waltham, Hampshire, were both 31 years old, and had a one-year old son, William.

8 High Street where Dr. Hale had his surgery, three doors down from 5 High Street (Past Historic Archive)

Dr Hale dismissed Mary Elphick's tales of ghosts, suggesting that ghost stories were a good way of keeping the Customs men from searching houses for smuggled contraband, or 'to cover the murder of an accomplice who knew too much'. What Mrs Elphick could have told the young couple was that smuggling had been a major problem in Hastings until around 1850, when low duties and an abundance of goods produced cheaply at home meant that there was little to be made by smuggling, and the practice decreased considerably.

Instead, Mary Elphick filled their heads with local stories of hidden chambers, hollow walls and floors, secret passages, double staircases and other smugglers' devices to fool the Excise men. Violet Hunt told the story of Mary's visit to a smuggler's home:

> She had been to stay once in a house opposite and was shown into a bedroom,
> but, when she opened a cupboard door to hang up her cloak, she found a bed
> of nasturtiums at her feet and the garden stretching all the way up the hill . . .

Apparently Gabriel and Lizzie enjoyed the stories, laughing at them for what they were.

If Violet Hunt is to be believed, then good, homely Mrs Elphick played a central role in caring for Lizzie during her stay in Hastings, calling the doctor when needed, feeding her as necessary and indulging her relationship with Gabriel in a most tolerant manner.

Some time in 1855, the Elphicks left 5 High Street as the tenants of Countess Waldegrave and moved very close by their good friends Thomas and Mary Elliot, who had rented 5 High Street before them and whose servant Sarah Veness had been. The Elliots had moved to 7 Carlisle Parade and the Elphicks went to Number 9. Later one of Sarah Veness's brothers, Thomas, moved into 10 Carlisle Parade. As always with the small town of Hastings, everyone knew everyone else.

John Elphick's health deteriorated and he died three years after Lizzie and Gabriel's visit. Mary reached ripe old age, surviving him by another 20 years. They were buried together in All Saints churchyard, with a fine headstone. Over the years the churchyard fell into disuse and graves became covered with vegetation, and the Elphick headstone disappeared from view. However, on 15 March 2003, I literally unearthed it from beneath grass and brambles. The stone had fallen face down, so that no inscription was apparent. My husband and I strained to heave it upright before the headstone yielded its secrets. It was clearly marked 'Sacred to the memory of John Elphick who departed this life June 13 1857 aged 64. Also Mary Elphick wife of the above who died Dec 19 1877 in the 88th year of her age'.

As described earlier, we organised the re-erection of the stone above its grave, and will ensure that it is known about by visitors to Hastings interested in the Pre-Raphaelites. Its rediscovery has added to Hastings's rich pastiche of Pre-Raphaelite connections. This, in turn, ensures that the small, but precious, part played by the Elphicks in the early happiness of Gabriel and Lizzie will not be forgotten.

The day after their arrival, Gabriel ensured that Lizzie was settled into her lodgings and then took himself back to London, where he had arranged lunch with John Ruskin at his Denmark Hill, Camberwell, home in order to discuss patronage. For different reasons, both men were pressured and it was an awkward meeting. Effie, Ruskin's wife, was leaving him for John Millais, with whom she had fallen in love. The marriage to Ruskin was eventually annulled on the grounds that it had never been consummated, then causing Ruskin maximum embarrassment. During the meal Gabriel was informed that his father was dying. This followed a prolonged illness and, although a sad loss to Gabriel, it was not unexpected.

Gabriel wrote briefly to Ford Madox Brown and William Allingham to let them know that Gabriele had died at 5.30 p.m. on Wednesday 26 April. Gabriel was torn in two directions. He was considerably anxious about Lizzie, but he could not leave London until after the funeral. Meanwhile, Barbara and Anna Mary had returned to the Hastings area and were staying at Barbara's father's Mountfield Farm at Robertsbridge. Gabriel wrote to Barbara to let her know that he would be in Hastings as soon as possible.

Gravestone of Mrs Elphick, landlady to Lizzie and Gabriel, and her husband John (Past Historic Archive)

In the meantime, Bessie and Mrs Elphick saw to Lizzie, who must have quietly familiarised herself with her surroundings during this time. Her upstairs room was to the right off a narrow corridor. It was about 3.80 m × 4.85 m (12 ft 4 in × 15 ft 9 in), with a central, typically Georgian window that overlooked the quiet High Street. As Lizzie looked out of the window on to the high pavement opposite, there was a gap between the cottages. Bessie Parkes had recorded in her Journal on 24 April the view that Lizzie saw. The gap 'reveals the West Hill, between trees rich with early spring – a fruit's Blossom . . .'

The light was from the northwest, a good light for artists, and Mrs Elphick had dressed the window with a half net curtain to take advantage of it. Such a view is obscured now by very tall houses blocking both the view and the light.

Violet Hunt's description of the layout of the house and the attic are basically correct. She describes the interior as:

The rooms and hall are papered the same, like a maid's cotton frock with the ghostly flowers of a hundred springs agone, meandering on a dun ground.

Wallpaper of the mid-nineteenth century from a closet under the attic stairs outside Lizzie's room (Past Historic Archive)

Following our discovery of an original upstairs closet, we found a layer of wallpaper there that *exactly* matches this description given by Violet Hunt. We had it dated by an expert to the 1850s and there is no doubt that it was the very wallpaper seen by Gabriel and Lizzie during their visit.

In Lizzie's room there was a small fireplace with a lit fire opposite the window and, in front of it, a reclining chair where Lizzie could stretch out and warm her toes. In one corner was her small bed and in the other was her little closet, which may not have given her enough space for her dresses. There was a wing chair and two small tables with two upright chairs in the window corners. A solid old oak beam looked down on her from amidst a white ceiling. It was companionably cosy, and allowed her to work in there with Gabriel when they were not exploring Hastings.

Meanwhile, in London Gabriel was fretting. Both Barbara and Bessie wrote to him saying that they were concerned for Lizzie, yet Lizzie herself wrote to Barbara on Wednesday 3 May, saying that she did not think her health was bad enough to go into a sanatorium.

That same Wednesday, Gabriele Rossetti's funeral took place. Still anguished, and with almost indecent haste, Gabriel caught the train down to Hastings afterwards and was reunited with Lizzie. He returned to the Cutter Inn.

The Cutter Inn, left, as it looked to Gabriel during his stay (Personal Collection of J. Ridd & P. Marsden)

The weather had become warmer and drier and Barbara remarked in a quick letter to Bessie that day, 'Today has been lovely and Hastings – that is the dear <u>dear</u> old East Cliff looked divinely beautiful . . .'. The lovely weather enticed Lizzie and Gabriel to the top of the East Hill, a considerably steep and long climb, which suggests that Lizzie's health had picked up on Gabriel's return. Barbara and Anna Mary Howitt met up with the young couple who, according to Barbara, looked 'so happy and cheerful that one could hardly believe anything of gloom or any form of death could be hovering near yet I still believe she is going fast'.

On the following day, Thursday 4 May, a concerned Gabriel wrote to Dr Wilkinson in London itemising all Lizzie's symptoms. On the same day Bessie and her friend Emma left Hastings, duty done for Lizzie now that Gabriel had returned. As always, Bessie was sad to leave the town she loved so much. Barbara and Anna Mary visited Lizzie and they walked together, being careful not to overtire her. The weather was glorious and lifted everyone's spirits.

While Lizzie was ensconced at 5 High Street, Gabriel had been staying at 'the Inn'. There he enjoyed the sea-views, noting that the sea 'today looks enamel in the sun' and 'Yesterday I saw the sun rise!!! over the sea – the most wonderful of earthly sights'. (Gabriel was never an early riser.) But he was not happy about being even a few minutes walk from Lizzie, and on Sunday 7 May he wrote to his mother that Mrs Elphick had found him a room for 8s a week, and that he would be moving into 5 High Street that day.

There are some clues that narrow down the possibilities of which room Gabriel stayed in at 5 High Street. The Elphicks slept downstairs in the parlour because of John's illness. Also downstairs were the dining hall, breakfast room and kitchen. There were two upstairs front rooms, one of which was Lizzie's, whilst the other was traditionally the parlour for lodgers. There were two back bedrooms upstairs, overlooking the East Hill, in one of which lodged Miss Von Esch, the music teacher. The other was presumably Gabriel's and was probably the room now converted into a bathroom. Had it been the other one, which adjoined Lizzie's, he would have heard her moving about through the very thin lath and plaster wall. Yet one morning he awaited Lizzie at breakfast and had to be told by Mrs Elphick that she was rising late. Because of the flimsiness of the walls, it seems unlikely that, while staying at Number 5, Lizzie and Gabriel would have enjoyed a sexual relationship without everyone else in the house being aware of what was going on.

Yet perhaps Violet Hunt was right when she said he was in the 'haunted' attic where there are two rooms, one large, one small. In a letter to his mother he said 'Barbara Smith said to the landlady how inadvisable it would be for her [Lizzie] to sit with me in a room without a fire.' The attic rooms had no fireplaces, so they would fit. Sarah Veness, the servant, would already be in the small attic room, so perhaps Gabriel was given the larger, but darker, one. Or it could be that he was saving money on the rent for his room by not asking for a fire to be lit.

Gabriel declared to his mother that Lizzie was 'apparently rather better than otherwise; at any rate not worse, either by her own account or by appearances'. 'No-one thinks it odd my going into the Gug's room (his pet name for Lizzie was Guggums), to sit there.' In other words, chaperoning did not apply here.

During this time Lizzie had started a study of 'Clerk Saunders' for a woodcut that she intended to do for William Allingham's *Book of Old Scots Ballads*, which he was editing for Routledge. The story of Clerk Saunders was written by Sir Walter Scott and told of the vengeful killing of Saunders by May Margaret's brothers, after finding the lovers in bed. It was typical material for a Pre-Raphaelite artist.

Monday 8 May was a windy day. It saw the young couple at Barbara Leigh Smith's brother's home, at Scalands Farm near Robertsbridge. Their father Ben had bought up land around that area, including Scalands, and it was at this farm that Gabriel and

Scalands, sketched by Barbara Leigh Smith (© The Mistress and Fellows, Girton College, Cambridge)

Drawing of Lizzie at Scalands by Gabriel (pencil, 1854, Dr Dennis T. Lanigan collection)

Lizzie visited Barbara and Anna Mary. They probably went by train and were fetched from Robertsbridge station, or walked to the farm not far away. The four friends roamed the gardens at Scalands and noticed that the wild irises were in season. They picked some and decked Lizzie's glorious tresses with them. She modelled for them, each of the artists drawing her in their own way.

Drawing of Lizzie at Scalands by Anna Mary Howitt (pencil, 1854. Mark Samuels
Lasner Collection, on loan to the University of Delaware Library)

Lizzie and Gabriel returned to Mrs Elphick's that evening, where Lizzie rested but
was very tired from the day's exertions. On Tuesday morning 9 May, she sent Mrs
Elphick down to Gabriel at breakfast with a message that she would 'not get up yet'.
Gabriel was in the middle of writing to Bessie Parkes. The letter was appropriately
written on black-edged paper and announced to Bessie the death of his father. As
Gabriel sat in the breakfast room with its wonderful morning light and enchanting
view of the East Hill, he wrote his thanks to Bessie for her continued care of Lizzie,
mentioning that he had written to Dr Wilkinson in detail about her symptoms.

Gabriel reiterated Lizzie's firm choice of not wanting to go into 'a place like the
Sussex Infirmary,' where, he continued, 'she would be surrounded by persons of

Drawing of Lizzie at Scalands by Barbara Leigh Smith Bodichon (pencil, 1854.
Mark Samuels Lasner Collection, on loan to the University of Delaware Library)

habits repulsive to her, and by scenes likely to have a bad effect on her spirits.' Gabriel was more than aware of Lizzie's need not to be shut in, and for her free spirit to be allowed to roam. Lizzie probably also felt that she did not want others to witness her retching and vomiting.

Two days later, on Thursday 11 May, Gabriel wrote from 5 High Street to his brother William, giving the latest bulletin on Lizzie's health, telling of the visit to Scalands and the 'most stunning country there'. He mentioned that there were 'several places tolerably within range hereabout which we ought to see . . . But Lizzie is not capable of too much exertion'.

Gabriel's letter to Bessie Parkes from 5 High Street. The black edging was because his father had just died
(© The Mistress and Fellows, Girton College, Cambridge)

However poorly Lizzie was at this point, at some time during their stay they did indeed visit other tourist sights. Every morning the two breakfasted and looked out over the East Hill. Given the extreme steepness of the gradient up several roads and paths from Number 5, Lizzie did well to manage the climb. Virtually opposite 5 High Street and still existing today, were rocky outcrops, out of which three arches had been carved to look like doorways. This was the nearest thing to a folly that Hastings had. Not only did they make the climb, made easier today by Britain's steepest funicular railway (built in 1902), but they had energy to carve their initials on to a corner of the rock. Sadly, sea breezes have completely eroded their efforts.

They also saw another 'visitor attraction' on the outskirts of Hastings – that of Old Roar. This was a waterfall that had been popular with visitors since Georgian times, when Hastings first became a seaside resort. In fact, that earlier resident of 5 High

The arches in the cliff during the eighteenth century, where the lovers carved their initials. They have long since weathered away (Past Historic Archive)

Street, George Wooll, had written and published a guidebook of Hastings from the house called *Picture of Hastings*, in which he described the walk through the ghyll to the waterfall. Since it was only 20 years between George Wooll's guidebook and Gabriel's visit, it is possible that Gabriel was aware of it. If not the guidebook, then Gabriel may have seen some of George's prodigious production of prints of the area, all published from 5 High Street. Although George could not have foreseen Gabriel visiting, it is pleasant to think that Gabriel may have been aware of George, and that 5 High Street linked the two writers and artists.

Gabriel was none too impressed with Old Roar. The old waterfall had dried up and no longer roared. Gabriel described it succinctly: 'the fall seems to have fallen so completely and successfully for we couldn't see it'. Neither did George Wooll before him hear the falls, and had to ask his friend 'if the old one was dead or asleep . . .'. George went on:

> The fall is between 40 and 50 feet over the perpendicular rock. Being rather dry it gave us a good opportunity of examining all round. We observed three or four chalybeate springs issuing out of the rock. We tasted the water and found it strongly impregnated.

George Wooll print of Old Roar (Personal Collection of J. Ridd & P. Marsden)

Gabriel made no mention of the spring or its taste, and yet they had actually gone to see the source of a stream that was visited by many for its health-giving properties. Hastings had the double advantage of having not only the sea but also the mineral waters to offer to invalid visitors.

Nothing daunted, Gabriel and Lizzie carved their initials on rocks close by. At present Old Roar is overgrown and unapproachable, but Hastings' authorities have future plans to restore the walk. There is no great waterfall though, so perhaps it will be renamed Old Whisper.

Friday 12 May was Gabriel's birthday, although he makes no mention of it in a letter to William Allingham from Number 5. He was 26. He noted too that Lizzie was better 'in some things', presumably meaning that her spirits had improved and she was less sick. She had now completed the woodblock for 'Clerk Saunders', which

Gabriel would take back to London with him. Although unstated, it is almost certain that Gabriel had made several return trips to London while Lizzie languished in Hastings. He was too active a young man to enjoy inactivity for long, as well as having continuing business to attend to in London.

Although Gabriel alluded to a second visit to Scalands, he gave no details, beyond mentioning that Barbara and Anna Mary had left for London. It was in this letter to William Allingham that he voiced his inner worries:

> Lizzie is a sweet companion, but the fear which the constant sight of her vary-
> ing state suggests is much less pleasant to live with.

Was he finding his role as nursemaid a difficult one to play? Certainly her frailty boded ill for normality in the future.

On Saturday 13 May the weather changed and became oppressively warm and windy, in spite of the cooling sea breezes that come every afternoon in Hastings. According to Violet Hunt, Lizzie again saw Dr Hale, who suggested that she moved from Number 5 to somewhere nearer the sea. Lizzie ignored his advice.

Gabriel wrote to his brother on Wednesday 17 May, suggesting that William should pawn a (tie?) pin of Gabriel's and send the proceeds to him quickly, as he was out of money ('Tin is no more.'). The rent was due to Mrs Elphick on the coming Saturday. In this letter he told William that Hastings was 'a stunning crib but rather slow'.

When he first arrived in Hastings, Gabriel had had several concerns – Lizzie's illness, his father's illness and approaching death, and his need to make an impression on John Ruskin for patronage. Lizzie had made some improvement, his father was dead and buried, and the patronage was secured. The relief of those three burdens meant that he was less stressed and could turn his attention to Lizzie and their stay in Hastings. He could have painted, but he had not taken his paints with him. However, he declared his indolence and did very little. He began to feel bored, missing the buzz of London, and tried to persuade William Allingham to come down and visit. He completed his drawings of Lizzie in her room and, according to Violet Hunt, Gabriel rearranged Mrs Elphick's furniture in the 'back room' in order to draw. He removed the whatnot from across the window, arranged plants on the steps down and posed Lizzie against them. This would only work if 'back room' meant the kitchen rather than the breakfast room. In 1854 there were no steps down from the breakfast room as there are today, but Gant's map of the time clearly shows steps down from the kitchen.

Whilst Lizzie spent much of her time indisposed, Gabriel would have had time to fill. He wandered the cliffs, and spent time reading letters received from his brother William, from Allingham and from Millais, and he replied to them. He would have seen those things mentioned in Violet Hunt's account – 'the fishermen's beach, dotted with net-huts and store-houses, high, black-tarred, gaunt, three-storied, built on pebbles . . .', all unique to Hastings even today and which Gabriel perhaps found of interest. Violet went on to tell of an old fisherman called 'Nunky', whose son had drowned in a lifeboat. There was a fisherman called 'Nunkum' Adams at the time of the young couple's visit, although no story of the lifeboat could be found.

Gabriel by his own admission confessed his lack of energy, announcing in a letter to Allingham that 'poor Miss Siddal has done ever better than I have'. One can but wonder how he filled his time whilst waiting for Lizzie to recover from her various bouts of sickness. Rossetti and Siddal authority Jan Marsh has suggested that Gabriel may have done so by writing poetry, or at least playing with ideas for later poems. Marsh felt that perhaps Gabriel had written *Sudden Light* and *Love's Nocturn* in Hastings because 1854 was the date given later by William Rossetti for these poems. Marsh said in a letter to me in April 2003:

East Parade, where Bessie Parkes stayed in 1854, on the seafront of the medieval Old Town, with the fishermen, the winches for the fishing boats, and the tall huts used for drying nets (Hastings Museum and Art Gallery)

If WMR's dating of 1854 for *Sudden Light* and *Love's Nocturn* is correct, then these poems offer themselves as candidates. [for being written at Number 5.] Their themes and moods are appropriate for this period in his emotional life, as he and EES went away from London together for the first time. *Love's Nocturn* invokes a lover sending telepathic messages to his beloved as she sleeps in such a way as to suggest that he might join her, in imagination at least.

Certainly Gabriel retained images of things seen in Hastings. On Monday 26 June he wrote to Allingham in picturesque language of the scenes of Hastings:

There are dense fogs of heat now, through which sea and sky loom as one wall, with the webbed craft creeping on it like flies, or standing there as if they would drop off dead.

In 1859 he was to write *Even So*, a poem not published until 1870 yet containing some of the same imagery as used in those halcyon days in Hastings:

But the sea stands spread
As one wall with the flat skies,
Where the lean black craft like flies
Seem well-nigh stagnated,
Soon to drop off dead.

This is surely proof enough that Gabriel worked on the drafts at 5 High Street.

Gabriel wrote ten letters from the house and it is hard to imagine him not having an equal number of letters in return. For Victorians, letter writing was the equivalent of today's telephone or email and there were several collections and deliveries a day. Gabriel may well have felt full of ennui, and isolated from his friends and from London, but in fact he was only at 5 High Street for a total of three weeks and three days from April to June. It has always been assumed that he stayed longer, but in fact it was Lizzie who stayed for approximately ten weeks, working on studies for 'Clerk Saunders', 'The Maid of Lockroyan', 'The Gay Goshawk', and a sketch to illustrate Gabriel's poem *Sister Helen*, as well as her sketches of a gypsy girl she met locally.

For Gabriel time was running out. He needed to return to London and continue painting, and was intending to do this in the latter part of May. At this point, though, Lizzie became unwell again and so he delayed his return to London in the hope that she would rally by the time he left.

It looks here as though Lizzie's health followed a pattern. She was very ill when she came to Hastings, perhaps triggered by Gabriel's dabbling with Annie Miller. Then she recovered somewhat while she had him all to herself, but, as soon as he suggested that he should return to London, she relapsed again.

Sadly, this was the cyclical pattern she would follow throughout her relationship with him. If the couple quarrelled, Lizzie would immediately distance herself by going away and her health collapsed in response. She would then get over it, patch things up and return to the fold in order for the same thing to happen all over again.

Some time between 27 and 30 May, Gabriel returned to London, but hastened down to see her on one occasion during that time. And he must have taken day returns during the next month. But how Lizzie passed her time is not known, other than working on her drawings – perhaps pining for him, perhaps drawing or visiting Scalands again and gathering her strength.

On Monday 26 June, Gabriel came to Hastings again in order to escort Lizzie home. In a final letter to Allingham that day, there is a glancing reference to the Hastings Town Crier, who was passing 5 High Street at that particular moment. This is an old custom in Hastings, dating from former times, and the town still has a Town Crier. Every year a competition draws Town Criers from other places.

The tiny town of Hastings had provided the young artists with a stage on which to play out their romance. By the time they returned to London, they were very much in love and still besotted with each other, as well as with the artwork that jointly consumed them.

5

The Intervening Years

Lizzie lifted a small phial of liquid to her lips and drank gratefully. At least she had this to help her with her difficulties. Now she would wait for the drug to take effect and once again feel the agony and discomfort leave her, as she drifted from pain-tinged reality to dulled disassociation.

What Lizzie was drinking was Laudanum, a Victorian soothing and consolatory cure-all. Laudanum was a tincture of opiate dissolved in alcohol, which would calm the never-ending stomach upsets and sickness and deaden the pain.

At some point, one of the doctors whom Lizzie had seen had suggested Laudanum for her – and unwittingly brought about the beginning of the end. The benefits of Laudanum were immediate and obvious. It relieved emotional as well as physical pain, creating a false serenity and inducing euphoria if enough were taken. It took the edge off depression and made the world look a better place.

Even amongst the working class Laudanum was used in cough medicines and lozenges, and it was common for children to be sent by their parents to the pharmacist or local grocer's shop for a pennyworth of the liquid.

However, the Victorians had no real conception of the extremely harmful effects of Laudanum – not of its addictive qualities, nor of the dependency it caused. For it to be effective, ever-increasing doses were needed as the body quickly got used to it. Nor was taking it seen as immoral or illegal.

And so Lizzie, through ignorance and desperation, became a drug user, an act that perhaps some would have seen as an indulgence, while others would have viewed it as a perfectly normal thing to do at the time given her state of health.

Laudanum, (lawd'a-num) n. opium dissolved in spirit or wine; some-times written Ladanum. [ing praise.

The dictionary definition of laudanum from *The Illustrated National Pronouncing Dictionary,* c. 1880s

With every stressful episode in her life, her condition worsened as she gradually increased the dosage until she was no longer able to control it. Rather, it controlled her. Consequently, Lizzie developed a drug dependency, which in turn affected her behaviour, causing mood swings from excitability to irritability and depression. She was already reserved, but now became withdrawn and unable to eat or sleep without first taking Laudanum.

As Gabriel blew hot and cold in the six years following their Hastings visit, Lizzie struggled to understand his actions and cope with his inconstancy. His behaviour was no doubt in response to her moods and ill health and he may or may not have attributed it to her taking Laudanum, but certainly he and others were aware of a change in her. Yet one wonders whether he truly grasped the ramifications of her unenviable situation.

Lizzie had become too ill to work and yet was not able to return to her family, who had their own problems. She could stay as she was, a model growing older and gradually losing her looks and earning potential, and too ill to go back to millinery or sewing, or she could go forward, learning to paint better, perhaps seeking patronage and accepting commissions, yet knowing she was not quite good enough for that without Gabriel's help.

Lizzie's only realistic option had been marriage and her only choice had been Gabriel. She had been fond of William Deverell, her discoverer, and found his early death devastating. Algernon Swinburne, the poet, had also liked Lizzie and was sometimes disapproving of the way the Gabriel treated her – more an object to be admired than a woman to be loved, he thought. Swinburne read to Lizzie on bad days, deeming her 'brilliant' and 'appreciative'. But she always continued to hope that Gabriel would face his responsibilities towards her and marry her.

What had begun for Lizzie as a romantic venture into a new and exciting world of art and artists became her living nightmare. At the centre of her tale of glamour, romance, betrayal and addiction was the man whom first she loved, then craved, then needed.

Lizzie felt disempowered by her status, depressed by her illness and jealous of other women to whom Gabriel came close. All this in turn triggered more attacks of her illness and more use of Laudanum, so that she could never bring herself to full recovery.

By comparison Gabriel was seen as a versatile high-achiever, confident, charismatic and popular amongst his own set. He was 'an unrepentant egotist' who led 'an unpredictable existence', thus making a close relationship with any woman a challenge, but more particularly for Lizzie given her own disadvantages.

There were certain traits in Gabriel's make-up that reflected an almost narcissistic personality type and which were exhibited in some of his behaviour. His self-confidence made him appear relaxed, yet he was extremely vulnerable if laughed at. He often flew into rages if things did not go his way and he vacillated between over-idealisation and devaluation. He obsessively idealised love, first with Dante's Beatrice, then with Lizzie and later with Jane Morris (William's wife), yet he took eight years to commit himself to marrying Lizzie. Whether it was the idea of marriage itself or of marrying Lizzie that was difficult for him is hard to tell, but it certainly had its roots in commitment issues. When he finally did commit himself, the proposal was less about love and more promoted by remorse and the possibility of Lizzie's dying.

Commitment and settled relationships had not been part of Gabriel's plans, whereas they had always been part of Lizzie's aspirations. This was a typical Victorian woman's need for security and without it she had little standing.

Lizzie struggled, with Gabriel's help, to become a working woman artist. Her case was most unusual. Whilst most aspiring artists came from the middle class and were

Some of the books on the Pre-Raphaelites collected by the author

men, Lizzie was a working-class girl who mixed with, and became accepted by, the PRB's middle-class circle of friends, until she herself became middle class too. Gabriel had by this time come to know John Ruskin, the famous art critic who had spoken out for the PRB in its infancy and had championed its cause publicly. Ruskin was an influential man. Helen Birchall, of the Ruskin programme, Lancaster University has written:

> He left behind 250 publications, over one thousand drawings and a wealth of letters and diaries. He is now considered a Victorian polymath, having exercised enormous influence over art, politics, science and culture in the second half of the nineteenth century . . .

Thanks to Ruskin, the suggestion of going back to nature and painting out of doors permeated much of the art of the century. Holman Hunt continued to be true to the Brotherhood aims, but the others broke away, Millais from the detail and Rossetti to paintings of large, sensual women.

With men, encouragement and support from Ruskin was no problem. Yet his dominating desire for perfectionism led him to criticise every woman who ever asked for help. Was he being misogynistic or just a typical Victorian male, who believed that art was a nice hobby for idle rich women? Ruskin expert Pamela Gerrish Nunn has written:

> Thus Ruskin's patronage, well meant though it may have been, often doomed its recipient to a much lower status than one hoped Professor Ruskin's wisdom might help her to attain.

Anna Mary Howitt was the victim of such an attack from him, and became ill and distressed after he delivered his opinion of her art.

Gabriel made John Ruskin aware of Lizzie's talent and Ruskin showed support for her in her endeavours by giving her an allowance of £150 a year. Ruskin's patronage was both a boon and an inconvenience. It meant taking his advice and painting as he suggested, but for Lizzie there was a problem. Ruskin and most other Victorian men did not support the consideration that a woman should make a living and support herself from art, or even work in the first place, and so women artists were never viewed seriously.

Although Ruskin seemed fond of her, and nicknamed her Ida, he would surely not have seen Lizzie's naïve paintings as great works of art. So why did he offer her patronage? The answer has more to do with offering her support whilst she recovered, thus taking the pressure off Gabriel. Ruskin feared that her illness was distracting Gabriel and he was concerned that this budding artist would sacrifice his own career for the sake of caring for his inamorata. Consequently Lizzie was advised by Ruskin to go and see his friend Dr Acland in Oxford, and to Gabriel he suggested that he should marry Lizzie and settle down to his career.

After three years Lizzie refused the patronage. Perhaps the pressure to paint so that she could fulfil Ruskin's requests was too much for her. Perhaps her poor health defeated her and she felt unable to meet deadlines. Or perhaps she, being a free spirit, felt rather restricted in what she could do.

Whatever it was, as wilful and determined as ever, Lizzie went her own way. Perhaps she liked her patronage, but recognised it for what it was – a sop to Gabriel. She undoubtedly felt she was worth more than this. She was also secure now amongst the Pre-Raphaelite circle, which knew her as a model, painter and poet. They allowed women to work alongside them, and did not force them to stop painting once they married. Lizzie, however, was at a great disadvantage compared with the other women because she was not married to Gabriel, or even supported by him, so she struggled on, battling continually with her ill health.

From 1854 onwards, throughout the next four years, a pattern developed of frustration, conflict, escape, ambivalence and reconciliation, leaving both parties feeling guilty. However, by January 1858 an event had happened that changed Gabriel's outlook. He had met Fanny Cornforth, a voluptuous model used by Edward Burne Jones and William Morris, and was so attracted to her easiness of attitude that he began to see her and to paint her. For Gabriel there were no repercussions from any of his actions or behaviour, no ups and downs and no sickness. Life was on an even keel again and he felt rejuvenated. Fanny was a free and easy creature, with no hang-ups. Until recently she was thought to have been a prostitute, but new research by Ann Drewery, Julian Moore and Christopher Whittick in their article 'Re-presenting Fanny Cornforth' conclusively disproves that. However, when Gabriel used Fanny as his model in 1859 for 'Bocca Baciata' ('The Kissed Mouth'), Fanny's ripe sexuality said it all. Undoubtedly she had helped unleash Gabriel's true libido. She remained fond of Gabriel to the end, so much so, that within a few weeks of Lizzie's death, she was sharing his bed.

The painting marked the turning point for Gabriel and acted as a prelude to his obsessive painting of sensuous women that lasted till he died. The female images were repetitive, symbolic and self-absorbed, and they displayed both male and female characteristics, as though Gabriel had merged his idea of himself as a male painter with his creation of a female figure. Fanny Cornforth had enabled him to release his latent sexuality and it triggered in him a different way of painting from that which he had used during those repressive times with Lizzie, with whom only his spirituality had found freedom.

Previously with the PRB, Gabriel had developed a technique based on a flat, decorative early style of art, begun when he illustrated his poems. Throughout the 1850s, he produced a succession of watercolours that were small, strongly coloured images, inspired by medieval themes relating to the poetry of Dante Alighieri. It was these early paintings that brought him to the attention of John Ruskin and they gained Gabriel a growing circle of admirers. Further work by William Morris and Edward Burne-Jones focused on the Arthurian legend and the work of the poet Tennyson. After Gabriel met Fanny, this style was put behind him. Even when Fanny became too plump to pose for paintings, she was replaced by another model, Alexa Wilding, and paintings of a more demure nature followed, including 'Regina Cordium' and 'Sibylla Palmifera'.

In a review of Gabriel's paintings in 1883 in the *Gazette des Beau Arts*, Theodore Duret wrote:

> The woman imagined by Rossetti is a colossal being, having, on a massive neck, a strongly accentuated head, with prominent lip and an enormous head of luxuriant hair. This creature, a kind of sibyl, siren, melusine, has none of the delicate aspects of woman; she is nonetheless very living, and, when one has gazed at her for a long time, she becomes unforgettable; she exercises a sort of fascination, but mixed with disquiet; one is afraid to approach her too closely, one feels that if she took you in her arms, she would crack your bones.

Although written years later, this quotation captures the very essence of Gabriel's new era.

Lucien Pissarro, who painted in Hastings in 1914, described the women in Rossetti's paintings as 'richly-glowing, deeply-loving, long-throated, dense-haired, full-lipped' ladies. Whatever one thought of them, one could not but have an impression of them.

During 1859 Gabriel did not see Lizzie at all. Both had continued with their artwork, Gabriel slowly gaining recognition and Lizzie even exhibiting at a private exhibition while still contending with her illness. But still she could not give up Gabriel, or her art, or her frustrated hankering for marriage. In Victorian society, Lizzie's commitment to Gabriel made her unacceptable to other men. By modelling, she had committed herself. By working alone with Gabriel she had compromised herself. Now she was out on a limb and on her own. It had all started so promisingly in Hastings and for a while seemed set to continue, their souls truly meeting as they

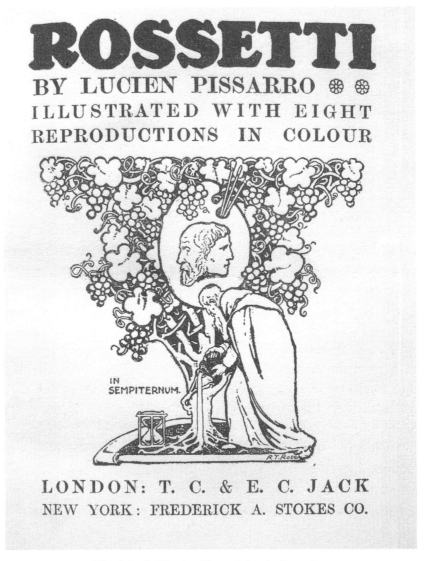

ROSSETTI

BY LUCIEN PISSARRO ✷ ✷
ILLUSTRATED WITH EIGHT
REPRODUCTIONS IN COLOUR

IN
SEMPITERNUM.

LONDON: T. C. & E. C. JACK
NEW YORK: FREDERICK A. STOKES CO.

The flyleaf of Lucien Pissaro's book, *Rossetti*

encouraged each other in their artwork and poetry. Lizzie's sorrowful, distressed, melancholic verse with its bitter-sweet poignancy must have offered her genuine solace, its composition soothingly therapeutic.

By 1860 the various pressures that bore down on her had conspired to make her very ill indeed and she was convinced she was dying. Her thoughts turned once again to Hastings and memories of happier times at the little house in the High Street, Number 5. Feeling desperately ill, helpless and hopeless, she made her way back to Hastings and willed fate to take its course.

6

Return to Hastings

Wishing she could die, Lizzie leaned over the bowl and vomited once again. All around her was the vile smell of sickness, and the sounds of her heaving and retching could be heard throughout the house. It was degradation at its worst and, far from recapturing old dreams, Lizzie was struggling with her very existence.

Probably she had felt that returning to Hastings would bring her closer to Gabriel and inspire some of those previous sweet memories of their happiest time together, but, when she arrived in the town, she was far too ill for any such pretensions.

During that first visit to Hastings in 1854, it was the landlady at 5 High Street, Mrs Elphick, who had so steadfastly cared for her. Mrs Elphick was a homely person, and Lizzie had felt comfortable with her. She had also witnessed the budding young love between Lizzie and Gabriel and had encouraged it. And so it must have been a shock for Lizzie when she decided to return in April 1860 to discover that Mr Elphick had died and that Mary Elphick had given up Number 5 and moved to Carlyle Parade.

With 5 High Street being unavailable, Lizzie would have remembered the only other accommodation she had known of – the Cutter Inn at 13 East Parade, where Gabriel had stayed initially. However, Lizzie did not stay there either, perhaps because it was too expensive or because it was full. Instead she took lodgings next door at 12 East Parade, where the landlady was Mary Chatfield and her husband was Alfred, a barber and hairdresser in West Beach Street close by. In most accounts of this second visit to Hastings, the Chatfields are not named, but are referred to as 'strangers' or 'unknown'. But Violet Hunt names the Chatfields and their involvement and, once again, her story checks out.

In 1851 Alfred (38) and his Scottish wife Mary (42) lived at 11 East Parade with their five daughters, Emma (13), Mary (8), Jane (6), Jesse (4) and Clara (3). By 1860, Mr and Mrs Chatfield had moved next door to 12 East Parade and were aged 48 and 53. They were now right beside the Cutter Inn. The Cutter Inn was rebuilt in 1929, across the sites of the by then demolished numbers 11 and 12. Today the inn carries a misleading plaque that says that Gabriel stayed there in 1860. In fact, neither Gabriel nor Lizzie stayed in the present building, but in the inn and lodging house previously on that site.

Since the Chatfields ran a lodging house, it is possible that they had some informal arrangement with the Dunk family who ran the Cutter Inn, to take any overspill if the inn was full. Maybe the Dunks had recommended the Chatfields to Lizzie. However it happened, Lizzie got to know Mary Chatfield and confided in her just as she had with Mary Elphick. Mrs. Chatfield certainly knew about her illness, for the noise of the vomiting could not be kept secret, and Lizzie must have told her about Gabriel as well.

The sickness perpetuated, and someone informed Gabriel that Lizzie was fatally ill. Despite not seeing Lizzie for about 20 months, he promptly went to Hastings to be at her side.

Full of pity and remorse, much affection and perhaps some love, Gabriel offered Lizzie the one thing she had sought since the beginning – marriage. He was finally cornered by circumstances. About to die was a woman with whom he had once been deeply in love and with whom he had shared much, yet paradoxically his erratic behaviour towards her had contributed to her present condition. Whether he genuinely loved her at this point is difficult to say. He had great warm-heartedness towards her and plenty of guilt, but was no longer in love with her, or in love with love.

Remorse was to be a familiar feeling for Gabriel – a pattern throughout his relationship with Lizzie of 'sin and repent'. However, this time it was different. Lizzie might die, so he did what he had to do – he offered her marriage if she would get better. At last Lizzie had the security that she so desperately needed, albeit at the eleventh hour. She accepted at once. Tellingly, Gabriel wrote to his mother 'Like all the important things I ever meant to do . . . this one has been deferred almost beyond possibility.' Remorse had made him clearly aware of his negligence.

Lizzie's condition at this time is a cause for speculation. Was she dreadfully ill and intending to die on her own? Or was the illness drug-induced, from taking too much Laudanum? It is thought likely that the latter is the most reasonable explanation. Or, indeed, was she genuinely ill and using the occasion to pull Gabriel back into her life again? She would have discovered early on that Gabriel was a compassionate man as well as a passionate one and that seeing her ill, especially after a long absence from her, would have affected his conscience deeply. So while he feared commitment, Lizzie's near-death state trapped him. This merry-go-round relationship game had already lasted nine years.

Gabriel wrote to his mother on Friday 13 April from 12 East Parade, where he was also lodging: 'The constantly failing state of her health is a terrible anxiety indeed; but

I must still hope for the best . . .'. Did Gabriel think that it would be a short marriage because Lizzie would die soon? Is that why he so impulsively gave Lizzie her heart's desire after nine long years of playing cat and mouse? Possibly, but he confided in his brother William on 17 April: 'If I were to lose her now I do not know what effect it might have on my mind . . .' and then: 'I must still hope for the best; indeed she has been as bad before in many respects, but hardly all at once as now.'

St Clement's Church, where Lizzie and Gabriel were married on 23 May 1860 (George Wooll print, Personal Collection of J. Ridd & P. Marsden)

The letter continued with details of obtaining a marriage certificate licence, and how Gabriel would have to speed back to London to pick up some money. He was also worried about the artwork he had been commissioned to do and when he would find time for it.

By 22 April Ford Madox Brown received a letter from Gabriel to say that Lizzie seemed 'ready to die daily and more than once a day. It has needed all my own strength to nurse her through this dreadful attack.' Then suddenly Lizzie began to recover, keeping down small quantities of water and beef tea, and was able to go downstairs. Gabriel noted 'this improvement is so sudden and unaccountable that one fears to put full trust in it . . .'. Emma Madox Brown offered to come down and look after her, but Lizzie wanted Gabriel and only Gabriel. Either she had got what she wanted, or she did not want anyone else to see her in this state.

They were hoping to marry on Gabriel's birthday on 12 May, but Lizzie was still too weak. Finally, they made it to St Clement's Church on Wednesday 23 May, 37 days after Gabriel's first concerned letter to his mother. The church was only three or four hundred yards walk from their lodgings, but it was on the top of a short, rather steep hill and involved walking up steps. Lizzie seemed to cope with all of this, and must have rejoiced as she stood at the altar of this lovely 14th-century church. The church had once been fired upon by the Dutch and still has a cannonball lodged in the outer wall of the tower. A copy of the ball was made and matched on the other side of the tower, and both can be seen today.

Gabriel and Lizzie were married by the Reverend Thomas Nightingale and their witnesses were two people who had featured a lot in their lives recently; Alfred Chatfield's signature is squat and black on the upper line of the certificate, and his 15-year-old daughter Jane's is small and neat underneath. Who better to witness the marriage than two people who were party to the struggle that Lizzie had so recently

Marriage record of Lizzie and Gabriel as witnessed by Alfred Chatfield and his daughter, Jane (East Sussex Record Office)

undergone in their house? The witnesses were not strangers, nor passers-by from the street, nor a couple, but a father and daughter who were part of their lives and had become a part of their story. The marriage certificate gives Gabriel's father as 'Gabriel' rather than 'Gabriele' and Charles Siddall is shown as an 'Optician'. This could have been a piece of inverse snobbery on Lizzie and Gabriel's part, an attempt to level up their class difference. The parish register recorded 'Dante' as 'Daniel'.

Lizzie had gained enough strength for them to set off on honeymoon, but had 'fluctuating health'. They went that afternoon to Folkestone with the intention of catching a boat to Boulogne, where they stayed for several days. In a letter from Paris on 9 June to William Rossetti, Gabriel noted: 'Still I need not say what an anxious and disturbed life mine is while she remains in this state.' Gabriel was concerned that he would be unable to work and raise money if he continued in the role of nursemaid.

The time away together was a success, although Lizzie was often too weak to get up. They renewed their acquaintance with each other and rediscovered each other, their passion for art bringing them closer together again. It was during this time that Gabriel did a pen and ink drawing named 'How They Met Themselves'. He had started it in the 1850s, when he supposedly became engaged to Lizzie. Its strange doppelgänger images show a lady and her knight in a forest meeting images of themselves as they look on with fear and uncertainty. It suggests that Gabriel saw his future with Lizzie presaged by death and despair. Lizzie completed one known painting 'The Woeful Victory' as an illustration for Gabriel's poem 'The Bride's Prelude'. Their money ran out at the end of June, Gabriel having to pawn trinkets he had bought for Lizzie before they reached London.

Unsurprisingly, Lizzie's health deteriorated immediately on her return to London and the hot fetid air. Chatham Place was especially unhealthy, being so near the odious odour of the river, but summoning the strength to move would have been a problem for Lizzie. Edward Burne Jones (Ned) and his wife Georgiana (Georgie), younger friends of Gabriel from the Oxford days, invited the couple to Hampstead. At the time Georgie wrote: 'I know that I then received an impression which never wore away, of romance and tragedy between her and her husband.' Georgie also tellingly recorded Lizzie's increasing dependence on Gabriel with the words:

[Lizzie] did not talk happily when we were alone, but was excited and melancholy, though with much humour and tenderness as well; and Gabriel's presence seemed needed to set her jarring nerves straight, for her whole manner changed when he came into the room.

Lizzie apparently 'sank back in peace'. Undoubtedly, Laudanum had much to do with her swing from calm to perturbation.

During this time Gabriel continued to see, and paint, Fanny Cornforth. If Lizzie knew it, it added to her already disquieted state. If she did not, it was as well.

From the post-Hastings time onwards, the relationship was flawed and dysfunctional, and doomed to failure. Gabriel was a free spirit who, as Violet Hunt quipped, painted where he loved and loved where he painted, while Lizzie struggled with the exigencies of daily living.

By 1861 Lizzie was pregnant, and gave Gabriel more cause for concern than ever – in those days many women died in childbirth and Lizzie was not strong to start with. Once again though, happiness eluded her and she bore a dead baby girl on 2 May.

The author at the Rossetti family grave at Highgate Cemetery, London, showing the final resting place of Elizabeth Eleanor Rossetti, née Siddal (Past Historic Archive)

Gabriel had been warned by the doctor what to expect, but seemingly did not tell her, although Lizzie must have known when she did not feel the baby moving. One can barely imagine what desperate emotions these two underwent, Gabriel shouldering his loss manfully, surely aware of a great depression. It was from this point onwards that Lizzie gave up. Always a fighter, she slipped into post-natal depression and increased her daily intake of Laudanum to blunt her emotional pain. Her behaviour became even more erratic and more dependent. She would suddenly disappear from the company of friends. All around her she saw healthy families and normal life. Undoubtedly she felt she had failed in every way and she turned in on herself in her depression.

Gabriel continued his life as before, painting, seeing friends, and poor, sick Lizzie began to resent the time he spent away from her. He was kind and gentle, but he was used to a faster pace of life. By this time he was no longer in love with her, and probably could not see past the sickness to the woman he once knew and idolised. He had a life to get on with and, although unquestionably cheerless after the stillborn

The inscription commemorating Lizzie on the Rossetti family grave at Highgate Cemetery, London (Past Historic Archive)

baby, he did not have post-natal depression. For him things were in focus. He needed to continue working to support his ailing wife and could not deny himself his friends' company lest he, too, lost his hold on reality. Nor could he deny himself the company of women as he continued his dalliances with Fanny. The status quo was becoming untenable.

The grave of Gabriel Charles Dante Rossetti at the churchyard in Birchington-on-Sea, Kent (Past Historic Archive)

Lizzie's was the most tragic of deaths. After she had dined out with Gabriel and Swinburne on the evening of 10 February 1862, Gabriel took her home because she felt particularly unwell. He went out again, some say to teach, some say to meet Fanny, and, on his return before midnight, could not rouse her. Beside the bed was an empty bottle of Laudanum that had contained two ounces of the drug. Taken all at once, it proved an overdose. Attempts to save her failed. Lizzie died by her own hand, whether accidentally or deliberately, successful at something at last. When William Rossetti visited to pay her his respects, his thought was, 'The poor thing looks wonderfully calm now and more beautiful.'

Gabriel was never truly able to get Lizzie out of his system. Between 1864 and 1870, he painted his wonderful 'Beata Beatrix' as a testimony to her memory, producing six replicas. Although he had affairs with other women, particularly with Jane Morris, he never married again. He became an increasingly pathetic figure towards the end of his life, plunging into despair and depression. He began to drink spirits and took an overdose of Laudanum in 1872. He became an addict to medically prescribed chloral hydrate in an ever-increasing attempt to combat insomnia. Sleep eluded his tormented soul as he dwelt on his memories and remorse took the edge off life. He found it progressively more difficult to paint, yet his works of art became better and better. He worked on paintings such as 'Proserpine' and 'Astarte Syriaca',

The inscription on the grave of Gabriel Charles Dante Rossetti at the churchyard in Birchington-on-Sea, Kent (Past Historic Archive)

powerfully beautiful images of tragic heroines, which sold for astonishing amounts of around £2000, about £136,000 in today's money.

Ironically, the more Gabriel's health slid into decline, the more his pictures sold for. He was now overweight, addicted, depressed and morbidly ill. He lingered for four more years, deliberately reclusive and deserted by his friends, until his death on 9 April 1882, a month before his 54th birthday. The end of his life mirrored the end of his unfortunate wife's in its degree of suffering, his unquiet mind perhaps repenting of his perceived wrong doing towards her one final time.

As time progressed, those early romantic times receded, leaving in its place one of the saddest stories imaginable of one of the greatest artists ever. Gabriel and Lizzie had lived and loved, and finally married, but real happiness had escaped them. Their personal tale is one of sad sequences and suffering – illness, depression, infant mortality, accidental death and eventual exhumation – the very stuff of dark tragedy. Their brilliance in art and poetry lives on in the writings of those who study literature and art history, and in the paintings and poesy themselves. But for those interested in reconstructing the historical aspects, it is the events of their personal lives and a curiosity about their relationship that attract attention – a relationship that deteriorated rapidly after the initial joyful explorations and discoveries of each other within the modest surroundings of the old house at 5 High Street, Hastings.

Select Bibliography

Adams, Steven: *The Art of the Pre-Raphaelites*. The Apple Press, London, 1998.

Ash, Russell: *Dante Gabriel Rossetti*. Pavilion Books, London, 1991.

Baines, J. Manwaring: *Historic Hastings*. Cinque Port Press, St Leonards, 1986.

Barrie, David: 'Ruskin Today', *Forum Quarterly*. London, Spring 2000, p. 7.

Barringer, Tim: *The Pre-Raphaelites*. Weidenfeld & Nicholson, London, 1998.

Belloc, Bessie Raynor: *In a Walled Garden*. Ward & Downey, London, 1895.

Best, Geoffrey: *Mid-Victorian Britain 1851–75*. Fontana Press, 1971.

Brodribb, Gerald: *Hastings and Men of Letters*. Old Hastings Preservation Society, Hastings, 1971.

Crompton, Margaret: *Prelude to Arcadia*. Unpublished Biography of the Early Life of Bessie Rayner Parkes. Girton College, Cambridge.

Daly, Gay: *The Pre-Raphaelites in Love*. Ticknor & Fields, New York, 1989.

Gerrish Nunn, Pamela: 'Ruskin's Patronage of Women Artists'. *Women's Art Journal* No. 2, Fall 1981/ Winter 1982.

Des Cars, Laurence: *The Pre-Raphaelites: Romance and Realism*. Harry N. Abrams Inc., 1999.

Doughty, Oswald & Wahl, John Robert: *Letters of Dante Gabriel Rossetti*. Vol. 1 1835–1860. Clarendon Press, Oxford, 1989.

East Sussex Record Office, Lewes, DGR's and EES's Marriage Certificate.

Faxon, A.C.: *Dante Gabriel Rossetti*. Abbeyville Press, London, 1989.

Forty, Sandra: *The Pre-Raphaelites*. Grange Books, London, 1943.

Gaunt, William: *The Pre-Raphaelite Dream*. The Reprint Society, London, 1943.

Hardin, Terri: *The Pre-Raphaelites. Inspiration from the Past*. Tiger Books International, London, 1996.

Hardwick, Joan: *An Immodest Violet. The Life of Violet Hunt*. Andre Deutsch, London, 1991.

Hastings Borough Council: The Gant Map of Hastings, c. 1850.

Hastings Reference Library: Local directories, maps, censuses and newspapers.

Hastings Museum and Art Gallery: Parish and family records.

Hawksley, Lucinda: *Essential Pre-Raphaelites*. Dempsey Parr, London, 1999.

Hawksley, Lucinda: *Lizzie Siddal: The Tragedy of a Pre-Raphaelite Supermodel*. Andre Deutsch, London, 2004.

Hilton, Timothy: *The Pre-Raphaelites*. Thames & Hudson, London, 1997.

Hirsch, Pam: *Barbara Leigh Smith Bodichon*. Chatto & Windus, London, 1998.

Hunt, Violet: *The Wife of Rossetti: Her Life and Death*. E.P. Dutton & Co. Inc., New York, 1932.

Lee, Amice: *The Life of William and Mary Howitt*. Oxford University Press, London, 1955.

Mancoff, Debra N.: *Flora Symbolica: Flowers in Pre-Raphaelite Art*. Prestel Publishing Ltd, London, 2003.

Marchant, Rex: *Hastings Past*. Phillimore, Chichester.

Marsh, Jan: *The Legend of Elizabeth Siddal*. Quartet Books, London, 1989.

Marsh, Jan: *The Pre-Raphaelite Sisterhood*. Quartet Books, London, 1989.

Marsh, Jan: *Elizabeth Siddal: Pre-Raphaelite Artist 1829–1862*. The Ruskin Gallery, Sheffield, 1991.

Marsh, Jan: *Pre-Raphaelite Women. Images of Femininity in Pre-Raphaelite Art*. Weidenfeld & Nicholson Ltd, London, 1995.

Marsh, Jan: *Pre-Raphaelite Character Sketches*. National Portrait Gallery, London, 1998.

Marsh, Jan: *Dante Gabriel Rossetti: Painter and Poet*. Weidenfeld & Nicholson, London, 1999.

Marsh, Jan: *Dante Gabriel Rossetti: Collected Writings*. Weidenfeld & Nicholson, London, 1999.

Marsh, Jan & Gerrish Nunn, Pamela: *Pre-Raphaelite Women Artists*. Manchester City Art Galleries, 1997.

Parkes Papers: Bessie Rayner Parkes's correspondence with Barbara Leigh Smith Bodichon, BRP V 173, BRP V 180, Girton College, Cambridge .

Past Historic Charitable Trust: Letters from Jan Marsh to the Author 1998–2003.

Pissaro, Lucien: *Rossetti*. T.C. & E. Jack, London, n.d.

Prettejohn, Elizabeth: *Rossetti and His Circle*. Tate Gallery Publishing, London, 1997.

Prettejohn, Elizabeth: 'Fatal Attraction', *The Art Magazine*, Issue 13, Winter, The Tate, London, 1997.

Pre-Raphaelites and Other Masters: The Andrew Lloyd Webber Collection. Royal Academy of Arts, London, 2003.

Rossetti, William: *The Pre-Raphaelites and Their World. A Personal View*. The Folio Society, London, 1995.

Siddal, Laurence: 'The Sad Short Life of Elizabeth Siddal', *The Review*, Pre-Raphaelite Society, Vol. X, No. 3, Autumn 2002.

Surtees, Virginia: *Rossetti's Portraits of Elizabeth Siddal*. Scolar Press, Oxford, 1991.

The Society of Women Artists – Exhibitors 1855–1896, Vol. 1 A–D.

Thirwell, Angela: *William and Lucy: The Other Rossettis*. Yale University Press, New Haven, CT and London, 2003.

Thirwell, Angela: 'John Everett Millais, William Michael Rossetti and the Bird's Nest', *The Review*, Pre-Raphaelite Society, Special Issue, Vol. XI, No. 2, Autumn 2003.

Thomas, Frances: *Christina Rossetti*. Self-Publishing Assoc. Ltd, Worcester, 1992.

Thornton, David: *Hastings: A Living History*. The Publishing Company, Hastings, 1987.

Todd, Pamela: *The Pre-Raphaelites At Home*. Pavilion Books, London, 2001.

Toohey, Jeanette M.: *Pre-Raphaelites: The Samuel and Mary R. Bancroft Collection of The Delaware Art Museum*. Delaware Art Museum, Wilmington, DE, 1995.

Troxell, Janet Camp: *Three Rossettis: Unpublished Letters to and from Dante Gabriel Rossetti*. Harvard University Press, Cambridge, MA, 1937.

Troxell Collection: Letters of Elizabeth Siddal, Princeton University, NJ.

Trueherz, Julian, Prettejohn, Elizabeth & Baker, Edwin: *Dante Gabriel Rossetti*. Thames & Hudson, London, 2003.

Whittick, Christopher, Drewery, Anne & Moore, Julian: 'Representing Fanny Cornforth: The Makings of an Historical Identity', *British Art Journal*, Vol. 2, No. 3, Spring/Summer 2001.

Wojtczak, Helena: *Women of Victorian Hastings: Their Lives and Occupations 1830–1870*. The Hastings Press, Hastings, 2002.

Wood, Christopher: *The Pre-Raphaelites*. Phoenix Illustrated, Orion Publishing Group, London, 1981.

Wooll, George: *Strangers' Guide to Hastings and St. Leonards*. G. Wooll, 5 High Street, Hastings, 1832.

Wickham, Angela: 'From Prodigy to President – John Everett Millais and The Royal Academy', *The Review*, Pre-Raphaelite Society, Special Issue, Vol. XI, No. 2, Autumn 2002.